Social Security Law in Serbia

Social Security Law in Serbia

Second Edition

Senad Jašarević

This book was originally published as a monograph in the International Encyclopaedia of Laws/Social Security Law.

Founding Editor: Roger Blanpain
General Editor: Frank Hendrickx
Volume Editor: Willy van Eeckhoutte

Wolters Kluwer

Published by:
Kluwer Law International B.V.
PO Box 316
2400 AH Alphen aan den Rijn
The Netherlands
E-mail: international-sales@wolterskluwer.com
Website: lrus.wolterskluwer.com

Sold and distributed in North, Central and South America by:
Wolters Kluwer Legal & Regulatory U.S.
7201 McKinney Circle
Frederick, MD 21704
United States of America
Email: customer.service@wolterskluwer.com

Sold and distributed in all other countries by:
Air Business Subscriptions
Rockwood House
Haywards Heath
West Sussex
RH16 3DH
United Kingdom
Email: international-customerservice@wolterskluwer.com

ISBN 978-94-035-2602-7

e-Book: ISBN 978-94-035-2603-4
web-PDF: ISBN 978-94-035-2604-1

The Author

Full Prof. Dr Senad Jašarević was born on 5 January 1963 in Novi Sad, Serbia (ex Yugoslavia). He graduated from the Faculty of Law in Novi Sad in 1986 where he earned his Master's Degree (The Roles and Significance of Collective Agreements) and his Doctorate (The Peaceful Resolution of Labour Disputes in Theory and in Practice). In September 1988, he accepted a position as a teaching assistant at the Faculty of Law in Novi Sad, where he currently holds the title of Full Professor, specializing in Labour Law, Social Security Law and European Labour Law. He is also visiting professor forPhD studies at the Faculty of Law, University of Mostar, Bosnia and Herzegovina. He served as Vice Dean for Financial Affairs (2002–2007). He is President of the Serbian Association for Labour Law and Social Security. He was a member of the Serbian Commission on the Democratization of the Educational System, the Serbian Government's Commission on Gender Equality. He is currently a member of the Employment Council of Autonomous Province of Vojvodina. Senad Jašarević was President of Statutory Council of the University of Novi Sad and President of the Ethics Committee of the University of Novi Sad. He is also the mediator/arbitrator of the Republic Agency for Settlement of Labour Disputes, and a member of the Restatement Group of the European Labour Law Network. He is the author of numerous scientific and professional works in the fields of labour and social security law.

The Author

Table of Contents

Table of Contents

List of Abbreviations

DFY (DFJ)	Democratic Federal Republic of Yugoslavia – 1943–1946 (Demokratska Federativna Republika Jugoslavija)
FPRY (FNRJ)	Federal People's Republic of Yugoslavia – 1946–1963 (Federativna Narodna Republika Jugoslavija)
FRY (FRJ)	Federal Republic of Yugoslavia – 1992–2003 (Federativna Republika Jugoslavija)
GDP	Gross Domestic Product
RS (RS)	Republic of Serbia (Republika Srbija)
SFRY (SFRJ)	Socialist Federal Republic of Yugoslavia – 1963–1992 (Socijalisticka Federativna Republika Jugoslavija)
Sl. l. FNRJ	Sl. list Federativne Narodne Republike Jugoslavije (The Official Gazette of the Federal Peoples' Republic of Yugoslavia)
SM (SCG)	Serbia and Montenegro – 2003–2006 (Srbija i Crna Gora)

List of Abbreviations

General Introduction

§1. General Background

1. The Republic of Serbia (RS) became an independent State after the dissolution of the State Union called 'Serbia and Montenegro' (SM) in 2006. This union was formed in 2003 and is considered to be the legal successor to the Federal Republic of Yugoslavia (FRY) which was formed in 1992 after the dissolution of the Socialist Federal Republic of Yugoslavia (SFRY). Serbia had the status of an independent kingdom prior to World War I. In 1918, Serbia became a Member State of a country that had a series of different official names, but is most recognizable to the world as Yugoslavia.

2. The RS is situated in the central part of the Balkan Peninsula. It covers an area of 88,361 km^2 and has a population of around 7.02 million. The capital city Belgrade, with 1,683,962 inhabitants, is the largest city in the State. The bordering countries are numerous: Hungary, Rumania, Bulgaria, Macedonia, Albania, Montenegro, Bosnia and Herzegovina and Croatia. The climate is mainly continental.

3. Serbia belongs to the group of countries known as 'countries in transition'. Its economy is in a deep financial crisis and its growing poverty and high unemployment present a particular social problem. There are around 416,600 unemployed people in Serbia, with the unemployment rate of about 15% of the active population.[1]

4. Serbia is very ethnically diverse considering that there are thirty-eight different nationalities represented within the country. Serbs account for the majority of the population (66%), followed by Albanians, Hungarians, then Romanians, Roma, Slovaks, Croats, Bulgarians, Turks and others. The official language is Serbian and the official alphabet is Cyrillic, but Latin orthography is also used. Orthodox Christianity is the predominant religion, but Islam, Catholicism, Protestantism, Judaism and other religions are also practiced.

5. From a geographical standpoint, Serbia can be described as the crossroads of Europe, due to its location on an important transportation route connecting Europe

1. According to official statistics, unemployment in Serbia is 12.9%, but in reality is higher. Statistics on unemployment can be seen on the site of the National Bureau of Employment (Monthly Statistical Bulletin), Internet: www.rztr.co.yu/bilteni/.

and Asia. Its three waterways, the rivers Danube, Sava and Tisa, are also of great importance to international transportation. The bountiful Pannonian Plain (stretching mainly throughout the province of Vojvodina) is located in the northern part of Serbia, whereas the central and southern parts are mainly hilly and mountainous. The largest proportion of land, 55%, is fertile while 27% is woodlands.

6. Serbian economy relies mainly on light industry (75.18%), but mining, electrical energy production and food production are also quite important.

7. In accordance with the Serbian Constitution adopted on 10 November 2006 (The Official Gazette of the RS, No. 98/2006), the constituent bodies of the Republic are the National Parliament, the President, the Government, the Courts (among them the Constitutional Court and the Supreme Cassation Court), the Public Prosecutors Office and the National Bank. By the Constitution, a particular characteristic of Serbia is that it contains two autonomous provinces – Vojvodina and Kosovo.

§2. Historical Background

8. The beginning of intensive development of the social security system in Serbia started at the beginning of the twentieth century as the country became more industrialized. In the nineteenth century, some forms of compulsory social security existed, but these were designed to protect only a few categories of workers and did not cover all social risks as well. This is probably why workers' 'mutual aid societies' were quite advanced and active in Serbia in the nineteenth century.

9. The first type of compulsory social security on Serbian territory was introduced in its northern province, Vojvodina, at the end of the nineteenth century.[2] At that time Vojvodina was part of the Austria-Hungarian monarchy, which was one of the first countries in the world to establish compulsory social security, in 1887. On the territory of Vojvodina, social security was limited to agricultural workers and applied only in cases of illness or injury incurred at work. This is why many uninsured workers founded 'associations for self-help' in the 1880s.[3]

10. In other parts of Serbia, at the time called 'the Principality of Serbia', the first regulations on compulsory social protection had already appeared in its first Constitution – the 'Sretenje Constitution' of 1835. In Article 137, there is a mention of retirement insurance for government officials, which was further elaborated upon

2. This insurance was regulated by legal Arts No. XVI from 1900, XIX from 1902, VIII from 1912 and XX from 1913.
3. Such associations were founded, for example, in Vršac in 1883, in Veliki Beckerek (today's Zrenjanin) in 1878, in Subotica in 1885.

in the Executive Order of 2 August 1841 on Pensions for Civil Servants, the Executive Order of 27 November 1843 on Survivors' Pensions and in the Act of 21 October 1871 on the Pension Funds for Widows and Orphans of Civil Servants. Additional legislation was passed in the nineteenth century, regulating the social security system to some extent:

- Executive Order of 14 August 1847 on Guilds (No. 1269).[4]
- Executive Order of 8 March 1841 on Free Medication for Low-Income Students (No. 156).
- Resolution of 20 October 1860 on Free Medical Treatment for the Poor (No. 175).
- Act on Mining of 1866.[5]

11. In addition, at the beginning of the twentieth century, compulsory insurance was introduced for State railroad workers, military staff and government officials. However, a large number of employees still remained without social insurance. This is why the creation of Mutual Aid Societies became widespread in the late nineteenth century.[6] In order to regulate this field, the State passed the Act on Mutual Aid Societies on 13 February 1902.

12. Great progress was made when the Act on Trades and Crafts Workshops was adopted in June 1910. This Act provided industrial and construction workers, as well as their families, with compulsory insurance in cases of illness or injury incurred while at work, and voluntary insurance in cases of permanent disability, old age and death. The insurance in the case of illness included free medical treatment and medication for the worker and his/her family, as well as salary compensation. In the case of disability, old age or the death of the head of a household, the family was entitled to financial aid or a pension. It is interesting to note that the law included financial aid for pregnant women, six weeks prior to and six weeks after giving birth. The financial costs of this insurance were equally shared between the employer and the employee. The system was administered by the State Fund for the Protection of Workers, which was made up of one representative from the State and an equal number of employers and workers. Unfortunately, due to the onset of World War I, this insurance society was never able to become fully operational.

13. After World War I, Serbia became part of the Kingdom of Serbs, Croats and Slovenes (later renamed as the Kingdom of Yugoslavia). Social security in Yugoslavia was regulated uniformly at the State level, so the individual system in Serbia did not have any distinguishing features.

---

4. This Act provided insurance to members of the guilds and their families in cases of permanent disability, old-age and death.
5. The Act on Mining stipulated establishing funds to subsidize miners and their families.
6. Those societies were formed by, for example, typographers, textile workers and workers in trades and crafts.

14. The existing forms of social security continued to develop in the provinces immediately after World War I. Under the pressure of workers' riots erupting throughout Europe (as well as in some parts of Yugoslavia) a few regulations, containing some forms of social security for certain groups of workers, were introduced. On 27 June 1921, the Executive Order on Social Security for Industrial Accidents and Occupational Diseases, insuring workers in the whole country from these risks, was passed.[7] Shortly thereafter, on 14 May 1922, the Act on Social Security for Workers was adopted, expanding social security, making it compulsory in cases of incapacity to work, old age and death.[8]

15. The Act on Social Security for Workers comprised of very progressive solutions for its time. The social security scheme was based on the German, so-called Bismarckian model, and the Act itself was drafted according to Austria-Hungarian pre-war legislation.[9] The Act envisaged compulsory insurance for all basic social risks; the widest possible material and personnel insurance coverage; insurance independent of salary; a unified social security system; and participation of both workers and employers in its management.

16. However, this social security system never became fully operational so that, prior to World War II, only 18% of Yugoslavia's population was covered by insurance. There were several reasons for this. First, only the illness and employment accident insurances were properly functioning in 1922, whereas the other types of insurance did not become effective until immediately prior to the war.[10] Second, the Act on Social Security for Workers (Article 4) and various special compulsory insurance regulations did not include many professions.[11] This prompted many groups of workers to create their own types of insurance schemes, thereby generating a very diffused and confusing social security system as a whole. The greatest problem was that no transfer of rights and/or investments between insurance schemes existed, and so workers who had changed jobs a few times never attained their right to a pension even though they had been paying contributions throughout their entire working lives.

17. Following World War II, Yugoslavia's borders remained the same, but the economic and political system changed. Socialism was introduced, bringing changes in the social security system as well. This system was set up in a manner consistent with that found in other socialist countries. One of the characteristics was

7. The Regulation was published in *Službene novine Kraljevine Srba, Hrvata i Slovenaca* (The Official Gazette of the Kingdom of Serbs, Croats and Slovenes), No. 184/1921.
8. The Law was published in *Službene novine Kraljevine Srba, Hrvata i Slovenaca* (The Official Gazette of the Kingdom of Serbs, Croats and Slovenes), No. 17/1922.
9. The draft of the Law was drafted in the tradition of the 'Austria-Hungarian Statutory Article', No. XX from 1907, which was in force in Croatia and Slavonia.
10. The pension and disability insurance only started operating in 1937 and unemployment insurance in 1935 – and then only very limited in scope. *See* D. Vukoviç, *Social Protection* 155 (The Centre for Social Work 1994).
11. For example, part-time (seasonal) workers, agricultural workers, fishermen and domestic employees.

that it aspired to institute an all-encompassing social security system under government support, based primarily on the solidarity principle, and not on contributions. This approach resulted in the achievement of a high level of social benefits, but later proved to exceed the real economic capabilities of these countries.[12] As a consequence, these social security systems fell into deep financial crises during the 1990s. The same thing happened to the social security system of the former Yugoslavia (the SFRY); it had been too generous in its scope of coverage relating to risks, persons and rights, and the benefits provided had been too great with respect to the invested means. This is the reason why just before the dissolution of the former Yugoslavia (SFRY), a reform programme aiming to rationalize the social security system had been launched.

18. Since the current social security system in Serbia is largely built on the old Yugoslav system, a few more words will be said about its development.[13] After World War II, the diffuse system inherited from the old Yugoslavia was in place – in all, 229 public and private social security funds existed in 1945.[14] Therefore, the first step that the new government took in this domain was to unify social security in 1945.[15] However, no fundamental changes in the system itself were made until the Act on Social Security for Workers, Clerks and Civil Servants was passed on 26 July 1946 (The Official Gazette of the Federativna Narodna Republika Jugoslavija (FPRY), No. 65/1946). This Act established universal compulsory social security for all workers and public officials, encompassing all social risks except for unemployment. The government assumed the responsibility to fulfil obligations related to social security through the State Institute for Social Security.[16] In addition, the conditions for attaining insurance rights in case of illness, old age and disability were moderated; medical treatment free of charge was established; material benefits in case of illness were increased and extended to cover a longer time period; the retirement age was lowered.[17]

---

12. *See* C. Gillion et al., *Social Security Pension: Development and Reform* 557 (International Labour Office 2000); and World Labour Report 2000, Income Security and Social Protection in a Changing World 135 (International Labour Office 2000).
13. During the period in question, such a large number of regulations were passed that a full account would take up too much space. This is why we will refer only to the most important acts and phases in the development of the system.
14. *See* R. Pešiç, *Radno pravo, knjiga III – Socijalno osiguranje* (Labour Law, Book III – Social Security) 240 (Faculty of Law in Novi Sad 1975).
15. This was done through the Decree of 30 Jan. 1945 on governmental supervision over social security funds, and the Act of May 1945 on enforcing social security. The Official Gazette of the Democratic Federal Republic of Yugoslavia *Sl. list Demokratske Federativne Republike Jugoslavije* (The Official Gazette of DFY), No. 29/1945.
16. This was done through the Decree of 30 Jan. 1945 on governmental supervision over social security funds, and the Act of May 1945 on enforcing social security (The Official Gazette of the DFY Sluzbeni list DFJ, No. 29/1945).
17. This was done through the Decree of 30 Jan. 1945 on governmental supervision over social security funds, and the Act of May 1945 on enforcing social security (The Official Gazetteof the DFY Sluzbeni list DFJ, No. 29/1945).

19. The next phase in the development of social security began with the adoption of the Act of 21 January 1950 on Social Security for Workers and Public Officials and Their Families.[18] This Act finally put workers and public officials on the same level in terms of social security rights. The scope of entitlements relating to illness and maternity protection was also expanded.[19] In 1952, a change was made in the way social security was funded: financing from the budget was transformed into a contribution system, which still applies. The capacity to insure certain categories of self-employed workers and the clergy was introduced the same year. It was also the first time unemployment insurance had been regulated; due to the post-war labour shortage, there had been no need for such measures up until that time.[20]

20. Also, a few words about the circumstances concerning other branches of social security after the war: family allowances were well established and highly developed from the outset. The first legislation in this branch, the Regulation of 27 April 1945 on Child Allowance,[21] had already been adopted during the war. At that time, in addition to the rights to child allowance, this branch of social security encompassed the rights of orphans to State care, a supplementary nutrition allowance for mothers and children, and single grants for families with many children.[22]

21. Minimum income protection was also established after the war. A more intensive development of this branch began in 1957, when the first institutions specializing in this area (centres for social work with children and families) were founded. These centres were later transformed into centres for social work, and today are the key institutions in this field for both federal units.

22. One of the unique features of the social security system in former Yugoslavia was that it paid great attention to the protection of war veterans, soldiers with disabilities and family members of soldiers killed during the war. The first Constitution of Socialist Yugoslavia of 1 February 1946[23] (Article 35) stipulated that: 'the State guarantees a dignified life and free vocational training for disabled veterans. Children of soldiers killed during the war fall under the special care of the State'. On 31 May 1946, the first in a series of legislative acts in this field was passed: the

18. Published in: Sl. list FNRJ (The Official Gazette of the FPRY), No. 10/1950.
19. For example, the right to material benefits in the case of permanent disability; in case of illness, material benefits were, in some cases, increased by 100%.
20. This insurance was introduced by the Executive Order on Material Benefits and Other Entitlements of Workers and Public Officials Temporarily Unemployed, of 31 Mar. 1952. *Sl. list Federativne Narodne Republike Jugoslavije* (The Official Gazette of the Federal Peoples' Republic of Yugoslavia), No. 16/1952.
21. The Code was published in *Službeni list Demokratske Federativne Republike Jugoslavije* (The Official Gazette of the DFY), No. 33/1945.
22. Over 1.3 million children were covered by some form of child protection in the period from 1945 to 1953. *See* R. Vukićević, *Socijalna zaštita u našoj zemlji* (Social Security in Our Country) 18 (Kultura 1962).
23. Published in: Sl. l. FNRJ (The Official Gazette of the Federal People's Republic of Yugoslavia), No. 10/1945.

Act on War Invalids.[24] According to this Act, war veterans had the right to a pension in case of disability, to third-party care allowance and to accommodations and care in specialized institutions.

23. The next phase in the development of the Yugoslav social security system began with the adoption of the following legislation: the Act of 8 December 1954 on Health Insurance (The Official Gazette of FPRY, 51/1954), the Act of 11 December 1954 on Retirement Insurance (The Official Gazette of FPRY, 51/1954), and the Act of 10 December 1958 on Disability Insurance (The Official Gazette of FPRY, 49/1958).[25] The aforementioned Acts brought about the separation of the health, retirement and disability insurance systems, making it easier to organize each branch. They also made provisions for many issues that are still applied today with only slight modifications. For example, the principle of unlimited validity of social security rights was established; a special contribution period for certain categories was introduced (*see* further); veterans' rights to pension facilities were included; disabled workmen were divided into three categories according to the degree of their disabilities; the notions of 'accident at work' and 'occupational disease' were precisely defined. Also, the possibility of obtaining voluntary social insurance for categories that had not been previously included in compulsory insurance schemes was introduced in 1956.[26]

24. In the period between 1961 and 1966, a series of legislative acts were adopted giving the Yugoslav social security system the profile and key elements that it maintained until the most recent reforms were developed in Serbia. Subsequent changes in social security regulations were less substantial and mainly organizational in character.[27] Some of the original elements for the time were the following:

- pension entitlements became more directly linked to the length and amount of contributions;
- conditions for entitlement to old-age and family pensions became stricter;[28]
- pensions were harmonized with salary fluctuations;

---

24. Published in: Sl. l. FNRJ (The Official Gazette of the Federal People's Republic of Yugoslavia), No. 46/1946.
25. These Acts were published in: Sl. l. FNRJ (The Official Gazette of the Federal People's Republic of Yugoslavia), No. 51/1954; Sl. l. FNRJ (The Official Gazette of the Federal People's Republic of Yugoslavia), No. 52/1954; Sl. l. FNRJ (The Official Gazette of the Federal People's Republic of Yugoslavia), No. 49/1958.
26. The Regulation of April 1956 on mutual aid funds (The Official Gazette of the FPRY, No. 15/1956).
27. From the more important regulations adopted in this period, the following should be mentioned: the Principle Act of 27 Dec. 1961 on pension insurance (The SFRY Gazette, No. 51/1961), the Principle Act of 10 Mar. 1965 on disability insurance (The SFRY Gazette, No. 10/1965), the Act of 5 Apr. 1965 on the financing and organizing of recruitment (The SFRY Gazette, Nos 15/1965 and 9/1970), the Principle Act of 26 May 1965 on health insurance (The SFRY Gazette, No. 24/1965), the Principle Act of 26 May 1965 on the financing and organization of social security (The SFRY Gazette, No. 24/1965).
28. For instance, the contribution period was increased to 40 years for men and 35 for women – regulations that are still in effect in Serbia and Montenegro.

- for the first time, insured persons were expected to participate in their healthcare expenses;
- regulations on professional rehabilitation were worked out in greater detail;
- basic rights regarding unemployment insurance, which are still in effect, were established (e.g., the right to material benefits, the right to free healthcare).

25. Toward the end of the 1960s, the process of political decentralization (so-called self-management) intensified throughout the country, creating a decentralization of social security as well. From then on, federal units regulated most of the branches of social security.[29] It is interesting to note that the provinces, Vojvodina and Kosovo, had their own parallel social legislation up until 1990 when they lost their legislative jurisdiction to the RS. The level of decentralization was slightly lower in the fields of pensions, disability insurance and the protection of veterans. Starting with the Act on Basic Pension and Disability Rights, adopted on 6 July 1972, these branches applied the principle whereby the State regulated only basic rights and conditions, while the rest was left to the federal units to elaborate upon.[30] Such distribution of jurisdiction in the aforementioned branches was in effect until the dissolution of the State Union of SM. The next federal law in this area was passed on 30 April 1982 and introduced the important policy of compulsory pension and disability insurance for the self-employed and agricultural workers.[31]

26. After the socialist system was abandoned in the early 1990s, reform of the social security system was undertaken, but has still not yet been completed.[32] Its long-term goal was to financially stabilize social security funds. Among other things, an attempt was made to strengthen the link between contributions made by insured persons and their entitlements.[33] One of the tendencies has been partial

29. The process of decentralization began in 1965 when the republics passed the first laws on employment. These were followed in 1967 by legislation in the domain of child protection also at the republic level, which is also when this branch finally broke away from the other social security branches. In 1970, both the republics and the provinces passed laws on health insurance.
30. The Federal Law with amendments was published in the Official Gazette of the SFRY, Nos 35/ 1972, 18/1976, 58/1976, 22/1978, 74/1980. After it had been adopted, the republics and provinces began to pass their own laws in these areas – Montenegro passed the Act on Pension and Disability Insurance on 29 Dec. 1972 (The Official Gazette of the Socialist Republic of Montenegro, No. 28/1972); laws with the same name were passed in Serbia on 16 Dec. 1972 (The Official Gazette of the Socialist Republic of Serbia, No. 51/1972), in Vojvodina on 31 Dec. 1972 (The Official Gazette of the Socialist Autonomous Province of Vojvodina, No. 26/1972), as well as in Kosovo on 28 Dec. 1972 (The Official Gazette of the Socialist Autonomous Province of Kosovo, No. 37/1972).
31. *See* the Act on Basic Entitlements to Retirement and Disability Insurance, published in the SFRY Gazette Nos 23/1982, 77/1982, 75/1982, 8/1987, 87/1989, 44/1990, 54/1990, and the FRY Gazette, No. 41/1994.
32. The most recent changes in this area were made in 2010 and 2014. Towards the end of 2010 and 2014, pension legislation was additionally reformed (Amendments to Pension and Disability Insurance of 2003, Official Herald of the RS, No. 101/10, 75/2014). Changes were introduced in the field of social protection (in the Act on Social Protection of 2011, Official Herald of the RS, No. 24/2011). Also, the Act on Health Protection of 2005 and the Act on Health Insurance of 2005 were redefined several times over the past few years (Official Herald of the RS, No. 57/2011).
33. For example, the Federal Act on the Basics of Retirement and Disability Insurance of 28 Jun. 1996 (The Official Gazette of the FRY, Nos 30/1996, 58/1998, 70/2001, 3/2002), which was in effect until

privatization of the social security system, that is, a combination of State and private (voluntary) social insurance. However, the changes were not deep enough, meaning that the social security system in Serbia is in a deep financial crisis today. This is why preparations for further reforms are currently underway in a number of branches of social security. In general, the system of social security has been made more practical and far more efficient over the years, however, owing to perpetuating economic crisis, the system itself is facing financial support issues.

§3. Sources of Social Security Law

I. General

27. When one considers the sources of social security law in Serbia after World War II, a few general observations can be made. First of all, these sources changed frequently, each time improving the quality of the system while maintaining the rights previously established. Second, the sheer quantity of legal acts regulating social security was (and is) extremely voluminous, making it very easy to lose one's way within the maze of regulatory rules. Third, each branch of social security has, for the most part, its own specific regulations. Fourth, following the war, social security was predominantly regulated through governmental acts and acts of executive power; however, a leading role in this field was later given to Acts of Parliament. Currently, laws regulate all fundamental and some of the more important issues, whereas technical and organizational matters are covered by regulations created by the executive powers and regulatory rules formulated by the individual social security institutions.

28. Higher authority above the law, as the source for social security governance, is the Constitution of Serbia (*see* above). It makes provisions for the basic socio-economic rights of citizens such as the right to social security, the right to health insurance, the right to social insurance, the right to the special protection of families, children and handicapped persons, the right to work and the right to an appropriate salary.

29. Collective agreements in this domain are of little significance for now, because almost all forms of social security are still in the hands of the State. Private social security schemes have only been initiated in the past few years, mainly in the field of health insurance and pensions. This has been followed by the introduction of private (supplemental) social insurance for the employees in a small number of collective agreements with employers (mostly in the public sector).

30. International sources of social rights play an important role. They can be divided into two groups: the first consists of accepted and ratified social security conventions and the recommendations of the International Labour Organization

---

2003, rescinded early retirement and introduced 50 years as the lowest retirement age, making it impossible to retire before then regardless of the individual's contribution period.

(over twenty conventions). The former Yugoslav legislation, as well as current Serbian legislation in this field is based on these sources. The second group consists of bilateral agreements. Yugoslavia has signed over fifty bilateral agreements on social security and employment with thirty countries. Serbia has generally accepted these agreements and has signed new agreements in the last few years. The largest number of bilateral agreements has been signed with industrialized European countries, as well as with countries bordering Serbia.[34] The aim of these agreements is to ensure better social protection for nationals temporarily living and/or working abroad; that is, to provide the same treatment for them as for the citizens of the country in question.

II. Legislation

31. The basic source of social security law in Serbia is the Acts of the Serbian Parliament. In addition, some former federal regulations are in force until the introduction of new legislation. Acts of Parliament regulate the all-important issues in this field, for each separate branch specifically. A unique feature is that the rights for all insured persons (wage earners, public-sector employees and self-employed persons) are regulated uniformly and largely in an identical manner. Moreover, the rights and the conditions necessary for entitlement to benefits are identical for wage earners and public-sector employees (excluding military staff and the police) while a few minor differences apply to the self-employed.

The following is a short, general overview of basic legislation on social security.

A. *Former Federal Laws in Force Only until the Adoption of Appropriate New Regulations*

32.

– Act on the Basic Rights of Soldiers, Soldiers with Disability and Families of Soldiers Killed during times of War, of 15 May 1998.[35]

34. Agreements have been signed with thirty countries: Austria, Belgium, Bosnia and Herzegovina, Belarus, Bulgaria, The Czech Republic, Slovakia, Ciprus, Croatia, Denmark, Egypt, France, Germany, Great Britain, Greece, The Netherlands, Hungary, Italy, Libya, Luxembourg, Macedonia, Montenegro, Norway, Panama, Poland, Romania, Russia, Sweden, Switzerland and Turkey. *See* Lj. Stojanoviç & V. Stošić, *Zbirka medjunarodnih ugovora o socijalnom osiguranju* (*Collection of International Treaties on Social Insurance*) (Zaštita Rada, 1996); S. Lakićević, *Penzijski sistem u Srbiji – osnovni koncept reforme penzijskog osiguranja* (*Pension System of Serbia – Basic Concept of Reform of the Pension Insurance*) (*Radno i socijalno pravo*, Udruženje za radno pravo i socijalno osiguranje Srbije i Intermex, 2008), No. 1, 507; *Implementation of International Agreements on Social insurance,* Ministry of Foreign Affairs, http://www.mfa.gov.rs/sr/index.php/konzularni-poslovi/socijalni-sporazumi?lang=lat, (10 Dec. 20015).
35. In Serbia, it is customary to cite the official publication from which a quoted Act was taken, as well as possible amendments to the Act, as these tend to be frequent. Therefore, when we mention regulations, we will cite the name of the publication in the footnotes. The above-mentioned regulations

B. Serbian Acts

33.

- Act on Health Protection, of 3 April 2019.
- Act on Health Insurance, of 3 April 2019.
- Act on the Protection of the Population from Infectious Diseases, of 24 February 2016.
- Act on Public Health, of 24 February 2016.
- Act on Patients Rights, of 22 May 2013.
- Act on Financial Allowances for Families with Children, of 14 December 2017.
- Act on Pension and Disability Insurance, of 2 April 2003.
- Act on Voluntary Pension Funds and Pension Plans, of 6 October 2005.
- Act on Employment and Insurance against Unemployment, of 15 May 2009.
- Act on Professional Rehabilitation and Employment of Persons with Invalidity, of 15 May 2009.
- Act on Social Protection, of 4 April 2011.
- Act on the Rights of Soldiers, Soldiers with Disabilities and the Members of their Families, of 25 November 1989.
- Act on the Rights of Civilian War Invalids, of 17 December 1996.
- Act on Determining Jurisdiction of the Autonomous Province Vojvodina, of 30 November 2009 (on the jurisdiction of Vojvodina in the field of social insurance and some other fields).
- Act on Contributions for Compulsory Social Insurance, of 24 July 2004.
- Act on Central Register of Compulsory Social Insurance, of 7 December 2018.[36]

III. Regulations

34. Formally, the domain of regulations is of secondary importance in Serbia. Their main purpose is to elaborate on rights that have already been established by law. However, from a technical and organizational standpoint, the role of sub-legal regulatory rules is indispensable. The social security system could not be practically applied without these rules.

---

were published in: (1) The Official Gazette of the FRY, Nos 46/1996, 12/1998, 37/2002; (2) The Official Gazette of the FRY, Nos 43/1994, 28/1996, 44/1999, 74/1999, 3/2002, 7/2005.

36. These acts were published in: (1) Official Herald of the RS, No. 25/2019; (2) Official Herald of the RS, No. 25/2019; (3) Official Herald of the RS, No. 15/2016; (4) Official Herald of the RS, No. 15/2016; (5) Official Herald of the RS, Nos 45/2013, 25/2019; (6) Official Herald of the RS, Nos 113/2017, 50/2018; (7) Official Herald of the RS, Nos 34/2003, 64/2004, 84/2004, 85/2005, 101/2005, 63/2006, 106/2006, 101/2010, 93/2012, 62/2013, 108/2013, 75/2014, 142/2014, 73/2018; (8) Official Herald of the RS, Nos 85/05, 31/2011; (9) Official Herald of the RS, Nos 36/2009, 88/2010, 38/2015, 113/2017; (10) Official Herald of the RS, Nos 36/2009, 32/2013; (11) Official Herald of the RS, Nos 24/2011, 32/2013; (12) Official Herald of the RS, Nos 54/1989, 137/2004, 69/2012, 50/2018; (13) Official Herald of the RS, No. 52/1996; (14) Official Herald of the RS, Nos 99/2009, 67/2012; (15) Official Herald of the RS, Nos 84/2004, 61/2005, 62/2006, 7/2008, 5/09, 52/2011,101/2011, 7/2012, 8/2013, 47/2013, 108/2013, 6/2014, 57/2014, 68/2014, 5/2015, 112/2015, 5/2016, 7/2017, 113/2017, 7/2018, 95/2018, 4/2019; (16) Official Herald of the RS, No. 95/2018.

35. Regulations stem from two basic categories: The first group is comprised of acts by the executive powers – governmental and ministerial acts (resolutions, codes and directives). The second group contains acts adopted by the social security institutions under the authorization of the State such as the respective statutes, rules of procedures, general resolutions, and so on.

36. The function of governmental regulations is to elaborate on legal rights, determine the scope of competence and define the procedural rules of the various organs. In this sense, acts passed by the appropriate ministries at the Republic level are more concrete and precise than the governmental acts. However, the whole system would hardly have any practical usage without the regulatory rules adopted by the institutions for social security and protection. A large number of technical and organizational issues relating to determining and attaining social security rights are regulated by such rules. Nevertheless, social security institutions are not allowed to interfere with the essence of those rights as established by laws.

37. Since over a hundred Acts belong to this group, we will mention only some of the more important ones:

- Executive Order on Health Protection for Workers, of 28 January 2000.
- Executive Order on Health Protection for Women, Pre-schoolers, School Children and Students, of 24 November 1995.
- Regulation on Particular Conditions and Means to Attain the Rights to Financial Aid for Families with Children, of 27 July 2018.
- Regulation on Conditions, Procedures and Means to Attain the Right to a Leave of Absence in Order to Care for a Child with Special Needs, of 18 July 2018.
- Regulation on Determining Occupational Diseases, of 14 March 2019.
- Regulation on Determining Physical Handicap, of 28 October 2003.
- Regulation on Jobs or Positions in Which the Term of Employment is Counted at an Accelerated Rate, of 28 October 2003.
- Regulation on Organization and Implementation of Pension Plans, of 1 July 2011.
- Regulation on the Content, Form and Procedure for Uniform Compulsory Social Security Applications, Uniform Methodology, Uniform Codes in the Main Registry of the Compulsory Social Security, of 4 August 2011.
- Statute of the Republic Fund on Pension and Disability Insurance, of 28 March 2008.
- Statute of the Republic Fund on Health Insurance, of 1 November 2011.
- Statute of the National Employment Administration, of 15 January 2010.[37]

37. These Acts were published in: (1) Official Herald of the RS, No. 4/2000; (2) Official Herald of the RS, No. 49/1995; (3) Official Herald of the RS, No. 58/2018. (4) Official Herald of the RS, No. 56/2018; (5) Official Herald of the RS, No. 14/2019; (6) Official Herald of the RS, Nos 105/2003, 120/2008; (7) Official Herald of the RS, Nos 105/2003, 126/2004, 93/2005, 3/2007, 8/2007, 56/2007, 23/2008, 49/2010, 48/2011, 50/2012 i 22/2013; (8) Official Herald of the RS, No. 48/2011; (9) Official Herald of the RS, Nos 54/2010, 124/2012, 119/2013; (10) Official Herald of the RS, Nos 31/2008, 37/2008, 140/2014; (11) Official Herald of the RS, Nos 81/2011, 57/2012, 89/2012, 1/2013, 32/2013, 23/2015; (12) Official Herald of the RS, No. 2/2010, 43/2011, 16/2012, 90/2015.

IV. Adjudication

38. The juridical system in Serbia is based on the principle of legality. This simply means that the Constitution, the laws and other general enactments are the only recognized general sources of law. Although court precedents do not formally represent a source of law, in reality the decisions by the Constitutional Court and Supreme Cassation Court have a significant impact, since the practical application of social legislation is dependent on them. More precisely, their decisions have a decisive influence on the proceedings concerning the administration of social security and the lower courts.

39. In Serbia, disputes in the field of social security are settled in Administrative Court through a special judicial process called the 'administrative disputes procedure'. This is actually the final instance to be applied to in these disputes. Only in some exceptional situations, the final word in the appeals process lies with the Supreme Cassation Court.[38]

40. In order for the public to be made aware of the practical work of the Supreme Cassation Court and other courts, important judicial decisions are published in a number of periodicals (*see* further, *Bibliography*) or on Internet presentations of courts. An alternative manner is to access the databanks of judicial decisions, which can be found in some databases on regulations.

V. Labour Agreements

41. As previously mentioned, labour agreements do not play a significant role in social security law because it is a topic that has, for now, barely been the subject of collective negotiations. The only issues that have been regulated by national collective agreements in Serbia until few years ago were:

– the amount of salary compensation in the case of temporary disability due to illness or injury;
– the amount of compensation during vocational re-training for persons with disabilities;
– severance pay in case of retirement.

42. With the development of private health insurance and voluntary pension schemes, labour agreements in the field of social security gained in importance because collective agreements started to regulate these social security issues more

38. Only disputes regarding health insurance are resolved by regular judicial procedures (in the first instance court decisions are brought by a Higher Court, while the appeals are settled by the Appellate Court). *See* Act on Courts Settlement, of 22 Dec. 2008, Official Herald of the RS, Nos 116/2008, 104/2009, 101/2010, 31/2011, 78/2011, 101/2011, 101/2013, 40/2015, 106/2015, 13/2016, 118/2016, 113/2017, 65/2018, 87/2018, 88/2018. Articles 23, 24, 29, 30. *See*: the Decision brought by the Supreme Cassation Court Us14/10, of 30 Nov. 2010, Belgrade http://www.vk.sud.rs/sr-lat/us-1410-sukob-nadležnosti.

frequently. Also, recognition of labour (collective) contracts in this field was encouraged by the new Act on Labour of the Republic Serbia of 15 March 2005.[39] Article 119 of the Code stipulates that the employer can make payments for the employees' voluntary supplemental pension insurance, collective insurance against consequences of accidents and collective insurance in case of serious illness or surgical interventions.[40] In accordance with this and the former General (National) Collective Agreement of 9 May 2008,[41] Article 34 envisaged that the employer can make premium payments for the employees' voluntary supplemental pension insurance, premium payments for collective insurance against consequences of accidents and collective insurance in case of serious illness or surgical interventions. Additionally, Article 35 of the same Act envisages that the employer is obliged to set aside at least 0.15% of the earmarked income funds for the prevention of disability at work. Although, this Act came out of force in 2011, the said provisions of the General Collective Agreement remained in use by the employers who have adopted them previously in the enterprise collective agreement.

39. Official Herald or the RS, Nos 24/2005, 61/2005, 54/2009, 32/2013, 75/2014, 13/2017, 113/2017, 95/2018.
40. Premium payments for voluntary pension insurance imply tax exemptions and contribution exemptions up to a certain monthly pension payment (around EUR 80). *See* Art. 13 of the Act on Contributions for Obligatory Social Insurance.
41. Official Herald of the RS of 9 May, Nos 50/2008, 104/2008, 122/2008, 8/2009. The legal outcome of this document remains uncertain. This collective agreement was signed for the period of three years. However, since social partners have not acknowledged extension of its validity, the collective agreement has formally ceased to exist on 17 May 2011.

Part I. The Institutions

43. The administration of the social security system in Serbia still operates mainly under the umbrella of the State. Even though private social security institutions are permitted to operate in most branches, there are few in existence. A number of private health insurance companies have been set up since the year 2000, and from 2007 onwards, in accordance with the Act on Voluntary Pension Funds and Pension Plans of 6 October 2005, seven private pension funds have come into existence.

44. The structure of State social insurance is fairly standardized. There is a ministerial department at the head, which is responsible for organizing and ensuring the proper functioning of the branch of social insurance under its jurisdiction. Some ministries are in charge of more than one branch. The management of each branch is conducted by separate and specialized social insurance institutions founded at the republic level (there are, however, no such institutions for all branches) (*see* further). However, at the local level, these institutions are composed of organizational units at the municipal level that are responsible for the implementation of the actual social insurance programmes. Certain services that fall under the jurisdiction of public institutions can also be carried out by private organizations (e.g., in the sector of healthcare services and social welfare).

45. Something unique in the organization regarding the social security system in Serbia is that the autonomous province of Vojvodina has, as of 2002, established its own separate social insurance institutions at the provincial level. These institutions are integrated into the larger insurance system of the Republic, but have generally replaced the central institutions in certain areas, such as the coordination and organization of local branch offices.[42]

42. *See* Arts 5162I, 65, of the Act on Determining Certain Competencies of the Autonomous Province. In the meantime, this law has ceased and now the Act on Determining Certain Competencies of the Autonomous Province Vojvodina of 2009 is being applied (*see* above).

Chapter 1. Public Institutions

§1. Ministerial Departments

46. The Act on Ministries of 24 April 2014 stipulates that social security falls under the jurisdiction of the following ministries:

- Ministry of Labour, Employment, Veterans and Social Affairs (in charge of issues relating to labour relations, also responsible for the implementation of social protection, child and family protection, pension and disability insurance, the protection of veterans and handicapped persons).
- Ministry of Health (organizes health protection and health insurance).[43]

47. The role of the ministries is to administer certain branches of the social security system and to ensure that the programmes are implemented in accordance with State policies. This is achieved through numerous means, such as directly applying laws and other regulations, as well as ensuring their implementation by passing appropriate follow-up acts. In addition, they are expected to instigate administrative and other measures, provide specialized help to the individual institutions, decide about certain rights of citizens and supervise the administrative work of social insurance and social protection institutions.[44]

§2. Public Institutions

48. Each branch of social insurance in Serbia has its own public institutions organized at the republic level, with headquarters located in Belgrade.[45] Central Social Insurance Register was set up in 2008. Its electronic database contains information on all payers of contributions for obligatory social insurance and to insured persons.[46] A specific feature in the Serbian system of public institutions is the existence of separate provincial institutions for health, pension and disability, and unemployment insurance, with their respective headquarters located in Novi Sad. Although these institutions operate with a high degree of independence, they are still subordinate to the central institutions.[47] In this way, the specific needs of the province Vojvodina are respected, without jeopardizing the system as a whole.

---

43. Official Herald of the RS, Nos 44/2014, 14/2015, 54/2015, 96/2015, 62/2017. The competencies of the aforementioned ministries were determined in Arts 15 and 16 of the Act.
44. *See* the Act on Government, of 27 May 2005 (Official Gazette of the RS, Nos 55/2005, 71/2005, 101/2007, 65/2008, 16/2011, 68/2012, 72/2012, 7/2014, 44/2014, 30/2018.
45. With the exception National Employment Service, whose head office is in Kragujevac.
46. *See* Centralni registar socijalnog osiguranja (The Central Social Insurance Register), http://www.croso.gov.rs/cir/index.php.
47. Provincial institutions are financially autonomous as well, since they have their own budgets. Also, their directors are authorized to appoint directors for local office branches within the territory of the province.

49. The social insurance institutions operate independently in their fields, but as previously mentioned, they operate under the supervision of the competent ministry. They function as special legal entities and manage their means independently within the framework of their jurisdiction. Their work is required to be made public.

50. There are, however, no specialized public institutions at the Republic level for social and child protection, the protection of handicapped persons, veterans, military and war invalids. These branches are administered either by local state administration or by municipal centres for social work, under the control of the Ministries. The services in this domain are carried out by various specialized social protection organizations.[48] Private institutions or individuals may also provide some of these services if they are equipped with the workspace, equipment and appropriate number of qualified personnel.

I. Overview of the Institutions

51. The most important public institutions in the field of social security are:

- Republic Fund for Pension and Disability Insurance.
- National Employment Administration.
- Republic Fund for Health Insurance.
- Central Social Insurance Register.
- Provincial Fund for Pension and Disability Insurance (for the Province of Vojvodina).
- Provincial Fund for Health Insurance (for the Province of Vojvodina).
- Provincial Employment Administration (for the Province of Vojvodina).

48. There are few kinds of state institutions for social protection. These are centres for social work, children and youth welfare centres, residential homes, retreat institutions, working centres, family accommodation and adoption centres, etc.

Chapter 2. Position and Competence of the Public Institutions

52. Even though they have great independence in carrying out their programmes, social insurance institutions have multiple ties to the State. They are formally autonomous, but their actual position is similar to that of State organs. The first area where State control can be recognized is that the ministries supervise the legality and skill with which these institutions carry out their work (inspections and other types of controls).[49] Also, in certain cases, if a person is dissatisfied with the decision made by the social insurance institution, he/she can appeal to the appropriate ministry.[50] Other illustrations of State control over social security institutions are, for example, the obligation of submitting annual progress reports to the respective ministries, or by having government influence in the appointment of members to management committees and by voicing their opinions regarding the internal regulatory rules of the institutions (the statutes, the annual budget plan).

53. The administration of the social security institutions is tailored to the particular needs of each individual branch. On the whole, their activities can be divided as follows:

- ensuring proper organization and implementation within their branch of social protection;
- establishing local networks of organizational units, and other bodies essential for successful implementation;
- precisely defining the procedures for exercising rights and ensuring their implementation;
- decisions concerning entitlements;
- maintaining essential records;
- monitoring new trends important in the implementation of insurance policies and planning for their further development.

54. The internal organization of social insurance institutions in Serbia is mainly standardized. As a rule, these institutions have two basic organs: an administrative board and a director.[51] Local units of social insurance institutions as well as social protection funds are, as a rule, managed by a director. A key role in appointing the management committee of social insurance institutions is played by the government, by selecting its members or approving of the composition of its governing bodies.

49. For each branch there are specially appointed inspectors – e.g., health inspectors, social security inspectors, work inspectors.
50. Appeals to the ministry are allowed in the fields of social protection, child protection and for the protection of handicapped persons.
51. The only exception is the Republic Fund for Health Insurance. This institution also embodies the supervisory board.

55. The management bodies of social security institutions are generally made up of representatives from the beneficiaries and the insured (wage earners and employers). In the last few years, considerable care has been taken to have these representatives elected by relevant bodies such as the most prominent professional or other organizations of the respective groups. For example, the administrative board of the Fund for Pension and Disability Insurance has seven members – among them are representative of the insured persons, representative of employers and representative of the beneficiaries. The representative of the insured is appointed by the most representative trade union at the Republic level, whereas the representative of the beneficiaries is appointed by the most representative association of pensioners of Serbia.[52]

56. Social insurance institutions are managed by an administrative board (or council). This organ adopts the statutes and other general regulatory rules of the institution; decides on the organization and the administrative hierarchy; determines the rate of contributions; makes the most important decisions regarding business policies, programmes, work plans, budget plans and annual settlement of accounts. It submits an annual progress report to its respective ministry, that is, to the Government.

57. The supervisory board is the internal control organ for social insurance institutions and mandated to supervise financial transactions, the implementation of the law, decisions made by the administrative board, and so on. Its composition is similar to the administrative board.[53]

58. The director of social insurance institutions leads and organizes the work, represents the institution, implements the administrative board's decisions and makes personnel decisions. Directors are lately being appointed in open public contests and according to the decision of the Board. Also, their appointment by the Board of the given institution is subject to the approval of the Ministry or the Government.

59. The administrative work for social insurance organizations is carried out by the respective administrative services of each institution.

52. *See* Art. 155 of the Act on Pension and Disability Insurance of Serbia.
53. In previous times, each institution of social insurance had its own supervisory board. Today, however, the existence of a supervisory board is expected only within the Republic Fund for Health Insurance. *See* Arts 19 and 20 of the Statute of the Republic Fund on Health Insurance.

Chapter 3. Private Institutions

60. Private social security systems have been relatively marginally represented, but they have gained in importance over the last few years, especially in the area of pensions.[54] The exception is in the area of healthcare services, where there have been noticeable developments within the private sector in the last decade.[55] Since there is presently an intensive economic privatization process underway, plans have also been made that would introduce partially privatized social insurance in the near future. It is expected that the role of private social insurance institutions will become more significant when the aforementioned takes place. This is currently hindered by low salaries of the employed, rendering them incapable of making supplementary contributions to a private pension or health insurance.

61. One of the reasons why private social insurance plans are not represented is that the population continues to trust State institutions more than they trust private institutions. The reason for this stems from the fact that the whole system has operated under State control for over fifty years. There is also distrust in private financial institutions, which is a consequence of the immense cases of graft and fraud that took place within the private banking industry in the last decade of the twentieth century.

54. Private pension funds have mostly been set up by major insurance companies or banks. Their operation and functioning is given under: *Penzijski fondovi (Pension Funds),* Narodna banka Srbije (National Bank of Serbia), Internet: www. nbs.rs/internet/latinica/62/index.html (2011); *Sektor dobrovoljnih penzijskih fondova (Branch of Voluntary Pension Funds),* Izveštaj za četvrto tromesečje 2017 (Annual Report for the Report for the Third Quarter of 2017), National Bank of Serbia: https://www.nbs.rs/internet/latinica/62/62_2/dpf_04_17.pdf; *Kamatica – Penzioni fondovi (Interest – Pension funds),* www.kamatica.com/investicije/penzioni-fondovi.

55. In the last few years, some private health insurance plans have been established, mostly by commercial insurance companies.

Part II. Contribution and Financing

62. The financing of the social security system in Serbia is based on the Bismarckian concept, meaning that payments are collected mostly from contributions made by persons working under employment contract and other persons whose income is based on the amount of work they do. A smaller amount of the financial resources, mainly for social protection, family protection and the protection of handicapped persons, comes from the budget.

63. The obligation to pay contributions applies primarily to the working population. The persons who fall under this category are mainly citizens of Serbia who are employed within the country but this insurance obligation also extends to certain persons outside of its territory as well as to foreigners employed in Serbia.

64. The legislation makes provisions for different employment statuses for different categories of workers; thus specialized contributional norms have been established for wage earners, self-employed workers and farmers. Various other differences have also been taken into consideration so that specific rules apply to persons temporarily working abroad, to foreigners working within the country and to domestic citizens employed by foreign employers. There is also a special category represented by persons hired for flexible types of work (high-school and college students, volunteers, temporary workers and underemployed persons, persons on fixed-term contracts).

65. A characteristic feature of social insurance in Serbia is that it is not financed from one joint account. Each branch (health insurance, pension and disability insurance, unemployment insurance) collects payments separately, but the method of collection is identical. Since 2004, the system of contribution payments has been regulated by a general Act for all branches of social insurance – Act on Contributions for Compulsory Social Insurance, of 24 July 2004. This Act has simplified the system of contribution payments since numerous exemptions, which thus far existed, have been removed. In addition, since then a proportional system of payment has been in use, which means that contribution payments for all insured persons are the same, and only the contribution bases vary.

66. In order to make the monitoring of contribution payments more effective, a Central Register of contributions for social insurance was set up by the Regulation on Central Register of Contributions for Social Insurance, of 25 April 2008.[56]

67. The Act on Contributions for Obligatory Social Insurance (Article 3) stipulates the following contributions:

(1) Pension and disability insurance:
  - contribution for compulsory pension and disability insurance;
  - supplementary contribution for persons with shortened periods of service;
  - contributions in case of disability and physical injury resulting from occupational injury and occupational disease.

(2) Health insurance:
  - contribution for compulsory health insurance;
  - contribution in case of occupational injury or occupational disease.

(3) Compulsory contribution in case of unemployment (insurance).

68. Funds collected through contributions are public revenue, are under the control and at the disposal of organizations for compulsory social insurance, and can be used only for purposes stipulated by laws on social insurance.[57]

56. Official Herald of the RS, No. 45/2008. This area is regulated by the Act on Central Register of Obligatory Social Insurance, of 7 Dec. 2018 (*see* above).
57. According to the Act on Contributions for Obligatory Social Insurance (Art. 4).

Chapter 1. Contribution Regulation for Employees

§1. Field of Application

I. Territorial Field of Application

69. The basic rule in Serbia regarding the social security system is that it is applied exclusively within its borders. Only in exceptional cases can entitlements be applied abroad (e.g., for medical treatment). Agreements with other countries on social insurance also contain provisions for some exceptions.

70. The question of who in Serbia is obliged to pay contributions is regulated for each branch of social insurance separately. However, there are almost no differences in the way this issue has been resolved for each branch. The duty to pay contributions is linked to employment or the performance of professional duties within the borders of the country. In other words, in order to be insured, the head office of the employer or the company of a self-employed worker has to be located on the territory of Serbia. Exceptions to this rule are persons working for a limited time abroad (détachè – posted workers) – they remain insured under the social security of Serbia unless they have mandatory insurance in accordance with the laws of the host country.

II. Personal Field of Application

71. The social insurance system of wage earners in Serbia is based on a system of contributions. Contribution payments are mandatory for all persons holding contracts of employment as well as for their employers. Contributions are paid by wage earners in all fields of work in the private and public sectors.[58] Domestic citizens employed by a foreign employer or an international organization in Serbia are also obliged to pay contributions. Also, unless otherwise stipulated by international agreements, foreigners employed by foreign companies on the territory of Serbia are required to do the same. The duty to make contribution payments also applies to domestic citizens working abroad, unless they have mandatory insurance in the host country, or if they are not entitled to any benefits outside the territory of the host country, in accordance with their laws.

72. The number of persons obliged to pay contributions for social insurance is greater than those included in the category of 'wage earners' according to labour law. In addition to these, as stipulated in the Act on Labour of 2005, the field of application extends to persons engaged in flexible forms of work, such as persons who work from home, persons on fixed-term contracts, household staff, temporary employees and part-time labourers. In addition, this obligation applies to some persons currently not working, such as:

---

58. These are persons working in companies, in the State administration, in local authorities, with other private employers, non-military personnel in the Army of Serbia, police and public officials.

- persons on leave without pay;
- persons receiving unemployment benefits;
- pension claimants;
- persons with a disability receiving compensation;
- persons receiving foreign pensions while residing in Serbia.

These persons are obliged to pay contributions only to the social security branches from which they benefit (e.g., retirees do not pay contributions for unemployment insurance). In addition to these persons, contributions are made by persons not obliged to be insured, but who are voluntarily involved in State social insurance.

73. In addition to the above, there are groups of persons not contractually employed. They still have to make contributions for insurance but only for accidents at work and occupational disease. These are:

- volunteers;
- unemployed persons undergoing vocational re-training;
- high-school and college students on apprenticeship;
- persons employed through youth and student associations;
- participants in public works and persons undergoing defence training;[59]
- persons incarcerated.

74. The Act on Pension and Disability Insurance in Serbia, of 2 April 2003 has introduced some changes in this area so that in this branch it is mandatory to insure the following, previously excluded categories:

- persons who have turned 26 years doing temporary and occasional jobs through youth associations or, regardless of age, those not receiving an education;
- persons on freelance contracts, authorship contracts or other contracts for which they receive compensation, while not insured on other grounds (these persons belong to the self-employed insurance group).[60]

75. The responsibility to collect and make contribution payments to the competent institutions lies with the employers. Other persons who are engaged in work for an employer and receive salary compensation, but are not employed permanently, are due to pay contributions if the employer fails to do that. The employer is obliged to do so for all employees, even if they are employed illegally or under an invalid contract of employment. There are no exceptions to this rule, regardless of whether the persons are employed part-time or full-time, or the kind of work in which they

59. As stipulated in the Act on Pension and Disability Insurance in Serbia of 2003, this group of individuals (as well as persons involved in emergency rescues or defence from natural disasters, at work camps, or involved in competitions) are insured only against injury at work but not against occupational disease. (Art. 254 of the Act.)
60. Articles 11 and 12 of the Act on Pension and Disability Insurance.

are engaged. Contributions have to be paid for the full period that a wage earner actively works or is absent from work due to reasons justified by labour law (e.g., due to illness or maternity leave).

76. Apart from the employer, the following are also required to pay contributions:

- temporary employment agencies – for persons engaged in temporary and occasional jobs;
- employment services – for the unemployed undergoing vocational education and training;
- the school, faculty or university – for students who are on professional apprenticeship;
- the state or local administration organization, institution, organization or employment service who engages volunteers;
- the other legal persons or employers if it is prescribed by social insurance legislation.[61]

§2. Calculation of Contributions

77. Social security contributions in Serbia have to be paid by all wage earners and their employers, as a percentage of wages. Half of the amount comes from the wage earner and the other half from the employer,[62] but it is the employer's duty to collect the entire amount and make the payments. For those temporarily inactive and at the same time enjoying social insurance benefits, contributions are paid by the competent institutions. For example, for persons receiving unemployment benefits, contributions are paid by the institution for unemployment insurance; for persons who are on temporary disability due to illness, contributions are provided by the institutions for health insurance.

I. Calculation Base

78. As a rule, the calculation base in Serbia is the effective salary payment or salary compensation according to the law and the collective agreement.[63] This calculation base is the same for all social insurance branches. Also, the lowest and

61. According to Art. 6 Act on Contributions for Obligatory Social Insurance: 'The onus of calculating and paying the contributions is on the insured and the employer or any other income payer who is obliged to calculate and pay the contributions in their name and on their own behalf or in their name and on behalf of the insured.
62. Regarding Pension Insurance, officially – employed pay 14% and employers 12% (although in practice the whole sum is paid by employers).
63. In order to prevent the avoidance of paying contributions, in 2001 it was determined that the wages, which are the basis for contributions and taxes, should include all other payments, even those that were in-kind, food allowances, and holiday pay. Prior to that there was a mass evasion of fulfilling

highest calculation bases have been established. The lowest calculation base is 35% of an average monthly salary in the Republic in the previous year, which is announced by the Republic statistics institution. The lowest monthly calculation base is determined and announced by the Finance Minister.[64] A calculation base ceiling has also been set – it cannot be higher than the fivefold average salary in Serbia.[65]

79. If an employer fails to make payments by the thirtieth day of the preceding month at the latest, he/she is obliged to pay contributions in the amount of the lowest bases set by the law. Later, when the employer has paid salaries, he/she is also obliged to calculate and pay full contributions.[66]

80. In addition to this regular calculation base, there are also specific calculation bases established for persons who pay contributions on special grounds:

- for persons in temporary or occasional employment as well as for those who work away from head office, the calculation base is a contracted amount;
- for persons working abroad for a limited time, the calculation base is the wage they would make performing similar work within the country;
- for domestic citizens employed abroad and foreigners employed by domestic employers, the calculation base is an average monthly salary in Serbia in the fourth quarter of the previous year;
- for foreigners who are employed by domestic employers on the basis of a special contract on the exchange of the experts or on the basis of the treaty on the international technical cooperation, the calculation base is an average monthly salary in Serbia in the fourth quarter of the previous year;
- for domestic citizens working for foreign employers, the calculation base is the net wage, wage bonuses and other salary compensation;
- for elected, entitled persons, the State officials who, apart from the salary earned with the employer with whom they are permanently employed, also earn additional amount of income while engaged in public work, the calculation base is the difference between these two amounts;
- for the insured persons who receive salary compensation because of illness from the fund of the obligatory health insurance, the calculation base is the amount of salary compensation;
- for wage earners on leave without pay, the calculation base is the wage he/she would make if actively working (it cannot be lower than that which has been determined by law);

---

obligations to the State and to social insurance institutions by means of disbursing various benefits in-kind and in cash that was disproportionately high in comparison to wages.

64. The lowest monthly contribution base in January of 2019 was RSD 23,921 (about EUR 202). *See:* The Amount of the Lowest Monthly Contribution Base for Social Insurance, of 28 Dec. 2018 (Official Herald of the RS, No. 104/2018). If an amount of contribution higher than the limit has been paid during a year, next year the difference is refunded in cash to the employee. *See* Arts 37 and 43 of the Act on Contributions for Compulsory Social Insurance.
65. *See* Art. 42 of the Act on Contributions for Compulsory Social Insurance.
66. Article 51 of the Act on Contributions for Compulsory Social Insurance.

- for pensioners' health insurance and for persons with a disability who receives compensation, the calculation base is the amount of their pensions or disability compensation;
- for persons receiving compensation for temporary disability or unemployment while undergoing vocational re-training, the calculation base is the amount of that compensation;
- for persons involved in compulsory social insurance the contribution calculation base complies with calculation bases imposed by the regulations of the organization for compulsory social insurance and which is approved by the Government of Serbia;[67]
- for persons receiving foreign pensions and/or for work invalids, the calculation base for health insurance is their net income for the month in which the contributions are paid;
- for persons on maternity leave allowance, the calculation base is the allowance;
- for persons insured only for the case of disability and body harm, for an accident at work or occupational decease, the calculation base is the lowest monthly base of contribution or an agreed-on compensation if it is higher than the minimum;
- for foreign citizens while on education or vocational training on the territory of the RS, the calculation base is an average monthly salary in Serbia in the fourth quarter of the previous year.[68]

81. Some other special rules apply as well. Special calculation bases have been established regarding pension and disability insurance for persons with shortened periods of service required to become eligible for pension (like pilots, policemen, military staff), whom employers pay additional contributions.

II. Contribution Amount

82. The contribution rates are regulated by the Act on Contributions for Obligatory Social Insurance, while the social security institutions do so only exceptionally, for specific groups of insurance beneficiaries (e.g., for voluntary insurance). Contributions are equal for private- and public-sector employees, as well as for self-employed persons. The only difference is that the contributions with private and public-sector employees are shared between the employee and employer, while the self-employed pay the total contribution themselves.

67. *See Osnovice osiguranja – Republički fond za penzijsko i invalisdko osiguranje (Calculation Bases* – Republic Fund for Pension and Disability Insurance), https://www.pio.rs/lat/osnovice.html.
68. *See* Arts 14–35b of the Act on Contributions for Obligatory Social Insurance.

Contribution rates for wage earners are:[69]

Branches	*Worker (%)*	*Employer (%)*	*Total (%)*
Pension and disability insurance	14	12	26
Health insurance	5.15	5.15	10.3
Unemployment insurance	0.75	0.75	1.5
Total	19.9	17.9	37.8
Contributions for Insurance for Persons Only Insured for Accident at Work and Occupational Disease	Employer (%)		
Pension and disability insurance	4		
Health insurance	2		
Total	6		
Rates for Pension and Disability Insurance for Persons with Shortened Periods of Service	*Additional Contribution Which Is Paid by the Employer (%)*	*Regular Contribution (%)*	*Total (%)*
when the effective twelve months of work are counted as fourteen months of contribution period	3.7	26	29.7
when the effective twelve months of work are counted as fifteen months of contribution period	5.5	26	31.5
when the effective twelve months of work are counted as sixteen months of contribution period	7.3	26	33.3
when the effective twelve months of work are counted as eighteen months of contribution period	11	26	37

69. *See* Arts 44, 46 and 47 of the Act on Contributions for Obligatory Social Insurance.

§3. REDUCTIONS AND EXEMPTIONS

83. On the whole, the general rule in Serbia is that nobody can be released from his/her obligation to pay contributions for social insurance.[70] Exceptionally, with particular categories such as, for example, freelance artists, priests and church officials, contribution can be paid by communal or district authority, Province, the RS or a cultural institution whose founder is the State.[71] The reason for the release is not explained, but it can be supposed that it is because of particular contribution to culture and spreading of faith.

84. Certain exemptions have been introduced in an attempt to bolster employment. In the Articles 45, 45b, 45v and45g, the Act on Contributions for Obligatory Social Insurance, it is stipulated that the employer is exempted from paying his/her part of the contribution, if he/she employs particular categories of workers permanently. Contributions are subsequently returned to the employer or they are exempted from paying them:

- for each new employee (till 31 December 2019);[72]
- if the employer or a small entrepreneur provides work engagement for two new employees (till 31 December 2019);[73]
- a disabled person is exempted for three years;
- when establishing a new company or an agricultural company (returns of contributions to the salaries of the founders of the company).[74]

In the aforementioned cases, National Employment Administration pays the contribution instead of the employer. The exemption does not apply to employers in the public sector.[75]

A person on leave without pay is temporarily exempted from the obligation to pay the contribution.[76]

---

70. This principle is explicitly emphasized in the Art. 64 of the Act on Contributions for Compulsory Social Insurance. Something similar is anticipated by Art. 115 of the Act on Tax procedures and Tax Administration (Official Herald of the RS, Nos 80/2002, 84/2002, 23/2003, 70/2003, 55/2004, 61/2005, 85/2005, 62/2006, 63/2006, 61/2007, 20/2009, 72/2009, 53/2010, 101/2011, 2/2012, 93/2012, 47/2013, 108/2013, 68/2014, 105/2014, 91/2015, 5/2016, 108/2016, 30/2018 i 95/2018.
71. *See* Art. 64a of the Act on Contributions for Compulsory Social Insurance.
72. In such a case, 65%–75%amount of paid contributions (including those paid on behalf of the employee) is returned to the employer in a separate procedure (the percentage of contributions money which is reimbursed depends on the number of employed workers). The only precondition to be met in order for the employer to get this refund is an increase of the number of his/her employees by 31 Dec. 2019. New employees in this context are unemployed persons or persons that have been registered with the National Employment Administration for six months, or three months (for apprentices).*See* Art. 45 and 45v of the Act on Contributions for Compulsory Social Insurance.
73. In this case, he is entitled to receive reimbursement amounting 75% of the security contribution paid. *See* Art. 64v of the Act on Contributions for Compulsory Social Insurance.
74. The reimbursement can be claimed on the income for the last twelve months, for no more than nine founders. *See* Art. 45g of the Act on Contributions for Compulsory Social Insurance.
75. According to Art. 45, para. 10, these financial incentives are not available to State organs and organizations, public agencies, public companies and services and state budget beneficiaries.
76. *See* Art. 48 of the Act on Contributions for Compulsory Social Insurance.

§4. 'TEMPORARY' NEW CONTRIBUTIONS

85. Considering that the economy of Serbia has been in deep crisis for a long period of time, it has not been financially feasible to introduce new contributions that would aim to stimulate employment or produce a financially consolidated social security system, as has been done in some European countries.

§5. CONTRIBUTIONS ON BENEFITS

86. The rule is that active workers pay contributions. However, there are exceptions to this rule, since some contributions are paid by persons temporarily or permanently inactive, while enjoying certain benefits from their social insurance. These categories pay contributions only for the branches of social insurance whose services they use (the responsible institutions do that for them).

Worker/Branch	*Pension and Disability Insurance (%)*	*Health Insurance (%)*	*Unemployment Insurance (%)*
Pensioners and permanently disabled workers	–	10.3	–
Persons on unemployment allowances or vocational re-training	26	10.3	1.5
Women on maternity leave	26	10.3	1.5
Persons receiving allowances for temporary disabilities	26	10.3	1.5

§6. ADMINISTRATION

87. In Serbia, employers are obliged to register every employee for insurance purposes with the competent social insurance institution, using the prescribed forms. The registration form for each employed worker is filed directly (in electronic form) to the Central Compulsory Social Insurance Register or indirectly, through the branch offices of the Republic Pension and Disability Insurance Fund and Republic

Health Insurance Fund.[77] All forms in each social security branch are to be uniform.[78] Insurance application records and the list of insured persons are kept in the Central Social Insurance Register of Contributions in identical form, and are to be submitted by the applicant in electronic form.[79] This uniform application has to be submitted three days after actual entering into the employment, i.e., three days upon signing of the employment contract or other forms of employment agreement, or as of the day commencement of work, the day of termination or cessation of work or working engagement or the day of an alteration made in insurance regulations. This uniform application sheet contains all relevant information required for the entitlement to the rights arising from compulsory social insurance, prescribed by the regulations governing pension insurance, disability insurance, health insurance and insurance in case of unemployment.[80]

88. The condition for exercising social insurance rights is that all contributions must have been paid. The contributions are paid to the competent insurance institution. In accordance with Serbian regulatory rules, the employer or other person having the obligation of paying contributions has to submit the proper form to the Republic Tax Administration and to the social insurance institution, showing the calculated amount of contributions due and proof of contribution payments. The Republic Tax Administration is responsible for controlling the contribution payments and has the obligation to inform social security institutions about contribution payments. The Republic Tax Administration and the obligatory social insurance organizations are also obliged to exchange the data relating to contributions.[81]

89. Decrees regulating personal income tax apply to the methods of determining contribution rates, interest rates and paying fines. Forced collection of contribution payments from legal entities is conducted in accordance with provisions governing the collection of corporate profit taxes.

90. Since huge problems have surfaced in connection with failure to pay contributions over the last few years, the Act on Contributions for Obligatory Social Insurance was introduced stipulating that the competent organ should initiate proceedings if the employers or other persons having the obligation of paying contributions neglect their obligations. They are to be fined. In the meantime, these

77. *See Centralni registar socijalnog osiguranja, Kako podneti prijavu (Central Register of Social Insurance, How to Register),* http://www.croso.gov.rs/lat/Kako_podneti_prijavu/index.php.
78. Insurance application procedure is uniform in each and every social insurance branch, as defined by Art. 12 of the Act on Central Register of Obligatory Social Insurance and the aforementioned Regulation related to the content, form and social insurance application procedure, of 2010 (*see* above).
79. *See* Uputstvo o postupku podnošenja jedinstvene prijave na obavezno socijalno osiguranje u elektronskom obliku i izdavanju potvrde o prijemu (Instructions on the procedure for filing a single application for compulsory social security in electronic form and issuing a receipt), Official Herald of the RS, No. 53/2013.
80. According to the aforementioned Regulation, Art. 2, this uniform application is designed so as to provide the following information: (1) general information on the insured person, (2) insurance details, (3) data on the contribution payer.
81. *See* Arts 70 and 71 of the Act on Contributions for Obligatory Social Insurance.

stipulations were extinguished.[82] In this case, according to the regulations in force, the Tax Administration shall initiate the penalty procedure (based on the Law on taxation procedure and tax administration).[83] Each and any avoidance to pay the tax is considered to be a criminal act that may imply up to three years of imprisonment for the employer as well as a fine. If the amount of unpaid contributions exceeds RSD 7,500,000 (about EUR 63,560), the prison sentence can reach up to ten years.[84]

82. Fines were stipulated in Arts 72–74 the Act on Contributions for Obligatory Social Insurance. Those stipulations were deleted from the said Act.
83. Stipulations related to fines are quite a complex matter so that they will not be elaborated in this context.
84. *See* Art. 226 of the Criminal Code of the RS (Official Herald of the RS, Nos 85/2005, 88/2005, 107/2005, 72/2009, 111/2009, 121/2012, 104/2013, 108/2014, 94/2016.

Chapter 2. Contributions for Public-Sector Workers

91. As previously mentioned, the status of public-sector workers in Serbia, in the domain of social insurance, is identical to that of wage earners. The same is true for social insurance contributions. Regulations referring to wage earners apply to public-sector employees as well. The only difference is that in this case, the State becomes the employer and is therefore responsible for performing all calculations and payments of contributions.

92. Military staff and the police are to some extent in a better position in comparison to other public-sector workers regarding social insurance benefits (e.g., their contribution period for retirement age is shorter). These benefits are financed from additional contributions, which are supplied by the State from the regular budget.

Chapter 3. Contribution for the Self-Employed

93. The logistics and administration of contribution payments for self-employed workers in Serbia do not differ from that of wage earners since the regulatory rules have been adopted jointly for all categories. Provisions were made only for possible aberrations regarding the method of determining calculation bases for contributions. This allowed for equal treatment of all employees with regard to social insurance, while at the same time specific characteristics of independent occupations were taken into account.

§1. Field of Application

I. Territorial Field of Application

94. Although it is not explicitly stated in any regulation, self-employed persons have the status of compulsory insurance holders only if they have been registered to conduct their business on the territory of Serbia. It is also implied that they should fulfil their tax and other fiscal obligations to the State on the territory of the Republic.

II. Personal Field of Application

95. All self-employed workers have compulsory social insurance unless they have been insured on other grounds.

96. With regard to contribution regulations, self-employed workers are divided into several groups, thereby recognizing the specific characteristics of each concerning both their social status as well as their ways and means of income. Most social insurance branches have established special calculation bases and rates of contributions for:

– founders and co-founders of companies, shops and other entrepreneurs;
– priests and other religious workers;
– farmers/ independent agricultural workers;
– freelance artists.

§2. Basis for Calculation of Contributions

97. The rule is that the calculation basis for contributions for self-employed workers is their net wage, that is, tax on profit or an estimated lump-sum income. However, since it frequently happened that workers in this category presented false income declarations in order to reduce their fiscal obligations to the State, a minimum contribution payments limit has been introduced (the same as for wage earners), which must be paid regardless of whether little or no income is received.

98. The basis for founders of companies and members of joint stock companies is the lowest prescribed monthly basis (*see* above), for entrepreneurs the base is wage. If they do not receive regular monthly salaries, the calculation base is an estimated lump-sum income (provisional lump-sum income as assessed by the tax administration). For the group of persons insured by means of a freelance contract or other contracts on the basis of which they receive compensation, the basis for pension and disability insurance is the contracted compensation amount for which income tax has to be paid. For freelance artists, the contribution base is tax on profit, but they can also choose to pay higher amounts of contribution.[85]

99. For priests and other religious workers, the calculation base is the lowest monthly base or an average monthly salary in Serbia in the previous year multiplied by the coefficient of 1–5. The height of the base depends on a priest's rank within the church hierarchy. The calculation base is determined by the church or a religious community in cooperation with a social insurance institution.[86]

100. For farmers (independent agricultural workers), the rules are slightly different. The lowest calculation base for which they have compulsory insurance is based on the earnings made from the agricultural work (which they pay to themselves), for which tax is paid. If they do not pay these earnings in a form of income, the calculation base for that period is the lowest monthly contribution base as for wage earners (*see* above).[87]

101. The contributions for these categories are paid in advance during the year, and the final account is made when their tax obligations for the year have been finally calculated.

§3. Amount of Contributions

102. Contribution rates for the self-employed in Serbia are the same as for other insured persons. There is only a technical difference. Self-employed persons pay the entire amount of the contributions themselves, while wage earners' contributions are shared between the employer and employee. The contribution rates for the self-employed are set in the following percentages:

85. *See* Arts 22–28 of the Act on Contributions for Obligatory Social Insurance.
86. *See* Art. 26 of the Act on Contributions for Obligatory Social Insurance.
87. *See* Art. 27 of the Act on Contributions for Obligatory Social Insurance.

Branches Workers	*Entrepreneurs (%)*	*Farmers (%)*	*Religious (%)*
Pension and disability insurance	26	26	26
Health insurance	10.3	10.3	10.3
Unemployment insurance	1.5	–	–
Total	37.8	36.3	36.3

103. No provisions have been made for reducing or suspending contributions for this category, except when self-employed workers temporary shut down their activities. The same is applied to agricultural workers – farmers.[88]

104. After they have accepted retirement, self-employed workers are no longer obliged to pay contributions for pension insurance and unemployment insurance, even if they continue with their professional activities. In other words, retired self-employed persons are allowed to continue their activities and combine them with their pensions.

§4. Administration

105. The administration in connection with contributions for self-employed persons is identical as for wage earners. Before 2008, the only difference was that special institutions dealt with administrative matters for this category in pension and disability insurance – the Republic Fund for Pension and Disability Insurance for the Self-Employed and the Republic Fund for Pension and Disability Insurance of Independent Agricultural Workers. Since 2008, all the Republic Funds for Pension Insurance have been integrated into one institution.

88. *See* Arts 49 and 50 of the Act on Contributions for Obligatory Social Insurance.

Chapter 4. Other Contributions

106. Apart from the three basic social insurance branches (health, pension and disability, unemployment) there are no additional types of compulsory social insurance in Serbia. Other branches of the social security system rely on government funding.

107. In the case that some persons remain uninsured, regulations in all social insurance branches allow these persons to participate in voluntary insurance plans with the State social insurance institutions (or with private insurance companies). They can choose between one or more social insurance branches. Also, by adding voluntary insurance to their compulsory insurance, all insured persons can expand the number of entitlement benefits. Financing of these entitlements is covered by additional contribution payments.[89]

108. However, due to the difficult financial situation of the majority of the population, additional voluntary social insurance with the State social insurance institutions does not really work in practice.

---

89. For persons voluntarily engaged in the State pension and disability insurance, the contribution base is determined by the pension fund when registering for the insurance. A person is entitled to choose one of thirteen offered solutions, i.e., bases, varying from the lowest that amounts to 35% of the average salary in the Republic for the past three months, to the highest amounting to five times the said average (i.e., from EUR 202 to EUR 2.895). Contribution base is the same as in other categories, i.e., 26%.

For persons engaged in health insurance, the contribution base is the lowest monthly contribution base determined by the law on contributions for social insurance. *See* the Ruling on Calculating Contribution Base for Persons Engaged in Compulsory Insurance of 2018 (Official Herald of the RS, No. 18/2018; Regulation on Calculating Contribution Base for Compulsory Health Insurance for Persons Voluntary Engaged in Compulsory Health Insurance of 21 Mar. 2006 (Official Herald of the RS, Nos 24/2006, 33/2007) and Regulation on the Means and Methods of Integrating Persons who do not have Compulsory Health Insurance in/to Compulsory Health Insurance, from 30 May 2018 (Official Herald of the RS, No. 44/2018). (Official Herald of the RS, No. 44/2018).

Chapter 5. Government Funding

109. Government financing in Serbia can be illustrated by the following:

(1) it makes additional payments for the financing of entitlements for persons with privileged benefits status;[90]
(2) it finances certain segments of the social security system from the general budget;[91]
(3) it subsidizes the resources that are lacking in some branches.

§1. Full Payment Out of General Taxation

110. Certain branches of social security are completely financed by the public authorities, without any usage of contributed funds. Those are all benefits connected to social protection (minimum income benefit and some other benefits for the poor), family allowances and the protection of handicapped persons (*see* further). These benefits are primarily funded from the budget of the Republic, but in Serbia there are also benefits that are funded out of the budgets of local communities.[92]

§2. Residual Funding

111. The State warrants compliance with social insurance duties. Should there be a deficit in the financing of contributions, the State is responsible for providing the additional necessary funding. These deficits have occurred quite often in the last few years, so the State had to subsidize around one-third of the pension payments. However, even with State subsidies, by the late 1990s, pensions for wage earners were overdue for several months, while agricultural pensions and child allowances were overdue for two years in arrears. These residual payments have mainly been covered by foreign subsidies after 2000, but it still happens that some payments are several months overdue (e.g., maternity leave compensation payments).

§3. Subsidies According to Fixed Criteria

112. Serbia has no ceiling on the amount that the State is allowed to subsidize social security benefits. So, there is actually no demarcation line between the responsibility of the State and the contribution payers in the financing of social

---

90. The State provides additional financing for wider benefits for persons who participated in war, for disabled veterans and military invalids, for civilian war invalids, for the police, for specialized health protection, for medical emergencies for foreigners and persons without citizenship.
91. Apart from the branches of social security that are financed from the general budget (which will be dealt with in the next paragraph), the pensions of exceptionally meritorious citizens are also financed by the State in accordance with special laws (e.g., ex-State presidents, ex-prime ministers, meritorious scientists, artists, writers, sportsmen).
92. *See* Arts 206, 208, 209 of the Act on Social Protection.

security. It is implied, however, that the insured are the ones who should cover the total funding of social insurance benefits through contributions. This premise has, however, been seriously jeopardized due to the economic crisis and the high unemployment rate. Since the subsidies for the social security system present too much of a burden on the national budget, it is expected that State subsidies will soon be restricted.[93] The same reason backs the plan to introduce a partial privatization of social security.

§4. Earmarked Taxes

113. Contributions and taxes represent the basic source of funding for the system of social security in Serbia. In addition to these, other supplementary sources of financing have also been established, such as:

- income from taxes on property belonging to social insurance institutions;
- income from dividends and taxes from insurance funds investments and financial transactions from issuing and circulation of bonds and shares;
- income from subventions and subsidies;
- income from the sales of public companies.

114. A significant deposit of funds is expected in this area from privatization in Serbia. Namely, a law has been adopted whereby pension and disability insurance funds are to receive 10% of all the proceeds from sales of State and public companies.[94]

115. Other, so-called alternative types of financing, from special taxes, fees or contributions, that have been introduced in some Western European countries (e.g., surtaxes on tobacco products, surtaxes on insurance premiums for automobile accidents, 'special crisis contributions'), are not being considered for now. However, those types of financing are indirectly being used for social security funding since the income collected from similar fees and taxes is used to fill in the deficit of the State budget. The State budget is used for pensions, health insurance and health protection and some social welfare benefits (*see* above).

93. For example, one third of the state budget is still used to subsidize pensions. *See Trećina budžeta i dalje za isplatu penzija (One Third of the Budget Continues to Pay Pensions)*, Politika (daily newspaper), 25 Apr. 2018, http://www.politika.rs/sr/clanak/402622/Trecina-budzeta-i-dalje-za-isplatu-penzija.
94. As stipulated in the Art. 17 of the Act on Privatization of the RS, of 5 Aug. 2014 (Official Herald of the RS, Nos 83/2014, 36/2015 112/2015, 20/2016).

Part III. Healthcare

Chapter 1. Field of Application

§1. Territorial Field of Application

116. In accordance with the practice in most countries, health protection is primarily tied to the territory of the country. This means that it applies mainly to State territory, that is, it is limited to insured persons who reside in the country. Exceptions to this rule are very rare; they exist only in specific cases that have been precisely defined by law.

117. Two laws adopted in 2019 regulate this sector in Serbia – the Act on Health Protection and the Act on Health Insurance, both of 1 April. In order for a person to enjoy health insurance benefits, a double territorial limitation has to be met: the beneficiary has to stay in Serbia when applying for and enjoying the benefits, and the benefits have to be provided in the State. To be sent abroad for treatment is possible only in exceptional cases. It can be approved only for insured persons if a medical committee concludes that successful examinations and treatment of the disease in question cannot be conducted in the country. The same applies to obtaining medication from abroad.[95]

118. There are special provisions for the health protection of persons working abroad as well. Those working for a limited time in a foreign country are entitled to the health protection in accordance with the bilateral agreement. The same applies to their immediate families (spouses, children). If there is no bilateral agreement with the country of destination, some Serbian citizens have a right to free health protection in case of a medical emergency. Those are Serbian citizens insured in Serbia but employed abroad, either with a Serbian or with a foreign employer, or with an international organization; persons sent abroad for the purpose of a short business trip or for continuing education or specialization, and to members of their families (with the exception of business trips). There is also a certain type of protection for private stays abroad (for tourists and similar). They are entitled to free health protection only in the case of a medical emergency.[96]

---

95. *See* Arts 11 and 72 of the Act on Health Insurance and Arts 2 and 9 of the Regulation on Conditions and Means of Referring the Insured to Treatment Abroad, of 15 May 2007 (Official Herald of RS, Nos 44/2007, 65/2008, 36/2009, 32/2010, 50/2010, 75/2013, 110/2013, 113/2014, 49/2016).
96. *See* Arts 111 and113 of the Act on Health Insurance.

119. For all of the above-mentioned persons, in order to receive free healthcare in a foreign country, a more general condition applies: prior to their departure abroad, it must be determined by the medical committee that in last twelve months they did not suffer from any acute or chronic illnesses that would require treatment or other medical attention.[97]

§2. Personal Field of Application

120. Those persons entitled to healthcare do not correspond exactly to those who have the duty to pay contributions; the scope is wider and covers a number of persons not subject to contribution obligations. Of course, the persons who do pay contributions are automatically entitled to benefits.

121. As in many other countries, because of its importance to society, healthcare is the branch of social security with the widest extension in its field of application. Actually, the list of persons covered by some form of health insurance is so extensive that we will not be able to list them all here – in accordance with the Act on Health Insurance, about fifty (fifty-three) different population categories have been included (around 92% of the population is covered by compulsory health insurance, while the number of healthcare beneficiaries is even larger due to the number of extensions).[98]

122. In addition to the basic contribution payers, active workers and self-employed workers, health protection is provided to temporarily inactive workers covered by various social benefits (during unemployment, disability, while receiving pensions). Health insurance covers their dependents as well – the immediate and extended family, as well as members of their household under the condition that they are supported by the insured person and are not otherwise insured. Additionally, to be covered by healthcare insurance, dependents need to meet some other conditions:

- the spouse of the insured is entitled to health insurance while married to the insured person;
- the divorced spouse who is, by court order, entitled to alimony is also entitled to health insurance;
- the child of an insurance holder is entitled to health insurance up to the age of 18, or up to the age of 26 if they attend university full-time or part-time, or are attending master studies;[99]

97. *See* Art. 114 of the Act on Health Insurance.
98. *See* Arts 11–23 of the Act on Health Insurance.
99. If the child remains incapable of living and working independently even after that age, and if the reason for being supported by the insured person is lack of income on the part of the child, the child is entitled to health insurance for as long as this condition lasts. *See* Arts 19 and 20 of the Act on Health Insurance.

- grandchildren, siblings, children without parents and children for whom custodial authorities have determined that they lack parental care are entitled to health insurance if they are supported by the insured;
- parents, step-parents, adoptive parents, grandparents are entitled to insurance if they are over the age of 65, or if they are younger but deemed completely incapacitated to work.[100]

123. In addition, as previously mentioned in connection with contributions (*see* above), health insurance against occupational injuries and occupational diseases has been extended to:

- students on apprenticeships or performing practical work in their fields;
- volunteers;
- young persons doing temporary work (up to 25 years);
- unemployed persons undergoing vocational re-training;
- participants in public works;
- participants in relief efforts following natural disasters and accidents;
- firefighters;
- persons undergoing defence training;
- persons involved in monitoring security at public events;
- persons serving a prison sentence if they are employed at the site;
- temporary workers in seasonal jobs.[101]

124. Also, health insurance provides persons belonging to groups considered to be more exposed to health hazards with health protection for the treatment of the most frequent and difficult diseases. These groups include:

- children up to 18 years of age, school children and students enrolled in school or university on a full-time basis, until the age of 26 at the latest;
- women in connection with family planning, pregnancy, childbirth and maternity (twelve months after giving birth);
- persons over the age of 65;
- handicapped persons;
- persons medically treated for contagious or serious diseases, monks and nuns;
- persons receiving minimum income benefits according to the regulations on social protection and the protection of veterans, military and civilian war invalids as well as the members of their families;
- persons receiving income benefits – members of families whose wage earner is doing military service;
- unemployed persons registered with the Employment Fund who are not receiving unemployment benefits;
- persons receiving regular financial aid whose head-of-household is away on military service;
- Roma without permanent place of residence;

100. *See* Arts 18 and 21 of the Act on Health Insurance.
101. *See* Art. 22 of the Act on Health Insurance.

- domestic violence victims;
- victims of human trafficking;
- victims of terrorism;
- war veterans.[102]

125. The resources for health protection in this category are provided from the national budget, unless secured by compulsory health insurance. The scale, content and method of their health protection are determined by the Government of the RS through special programmes within 'social concern regarding the welfare of citizens'.[103]

126. Owing to all of these extensions, almost the entire population is covered under State healthcare. However, due to the serious lack of financial resources, reality does not correspond to the regulations as they exist on paper. For some health services and appointments there is sometimes a waiting period of up to several months (and sometimes even up to several years), which defeats the purpose of the policy. Such incidents happen although they are explicitly forbidden by law. Article 129 of the Act on Health Insurance stipulates that for health services that are not urgent, a waiting list may be made ensuring that waiting times cannot be so long as to endanger the health or life of the insured person.[104] Also, some medical services are not available at all due to outdated, malfunctioning equipment or even the complete lack of said equipment, forcing the insured person to seek treatment outside the State healthcare system; seeking care with private practices or institutions. Unfortunately, a large part of the population cannot afford this kind of medical treatment, which is why a significant deterioration in overall health is evident.

102. *See* Art. 22 of the Act on Health Insurance.
103. In accordance with the Act on Health Protection (Art. 11).
104. Owing to these problems, amendments of the previous Act on Health Protection from July 2011 have introduced the 'Right to Respect for Patients Time' (by Art. 40a of the Act). This right is now regulated by a special Act which came into force in 2013 i.e., by the Act on Patients Rights. According to Art. 29, should the medical care fail to be administered right away, the patient has the right to make a check-up and diagnostic appointments, as well as other medical treatments in the shortest possible time. In practice, however, there is no guarantee that such procedures will be carried out in reasonable time as illustrated by the example of patients waiting for such check-ups and surgery treatment for several years. *See*: *KG: Surgeries to Be Procured in 2022*, Bliconline (daily newspaper), 13 Nov. 2013, http://www.b92.net/info/vesti/index.php?yyyy=2013&mm=11&dd=13&nav_id=777074; *Liste čekanja smanjene za 6.000 ljudi, ali se na operaciju i dalje čeka do 2023 (Waiting Lists Reduced to 6,000 People, but You Still Have to Wait for a Surgery Till 2023)*, Bliconline (daily newspaper), 9 Apr. 2019, https://www.blic.rs/vesti/drustvo/liste-cekanja-smanjene-za-6000-ljudi-ali-se-na-operaciju-i-dalje-ceka-do-2023/8ltrhfn.

Chapter 2. Benefits

§1. Care Provided

127. Health insurance in Serbia ensures two types of rights: a right associated with medical treatment, and certain material rights related to the illness (cash benefits). Under Article 49 of the Act on Health Insurance those are:

(a) right to health protection;
(b) right to cash benefits (due to (1) short- and medium-term incapacity to work; (2) transportation costs associated with obtaining health coverage).

128. Different types of 'medical benefits' provided by compulsory health insurance are regulated by Article 52 of the Act on Health Insurance. These include:

- medical procedures and treatments to improve overall health, that is prevention, treatment and early detection of diseases and other health problems;
- physical examinations and other medical appointments aiming to determine the general health condition of a patient and to provide regular control;
- treatment of the sick and injured and other types of medical assistance;
- preventive and curative dental care;
- rehabilitation;
- medication, medical aids and all medical supplies needed for treatment;
- prosthetic, orthopaedic and other support devices;
- medical auxiliaries, dentures and other dental care supplies.

129. This list shows the intention of the legislators to include all essential health services that can possibly be provided in the country. All cited services are primarily financed by health insurance. Local travel expenses in connection with health protection are not covered by the insurance, with the exception that for persons incapable of using public transport or for emergency cases, an ambulance is provided free of charge.

130. In addition to these healthcare services, the Act of Health Protection (Article 14) stipulates that employees are entitled to 'specific health protection' provided and financed by the employer. This type of protection includes:

- physical examinations to determine the capability to work;
- regular general check-ups;
- compulsory physical examination of employees for the purpose of environmental protection and the protection of the working environment, as well as consumer protection;
- introducing health protection measures at work for employees and their further education in the use of protective devices;
- sending those employees that are particularly exposed to health hazards at work on active leave for prevention of illness and/or early rehabilitation;

- other preventive measures (voluntary vaccination, voluntary general check-ups, evaluation of the health effects of the new equipment and technology, etc.);
- monitoring illnesses, injuries, absences from work, and death and other signs of possible health problems that affect work capabilities;
- providing first aid in case of an accident at work and providing conditions for urgent medical intervention.

131. Some healthcare services that are considered to cover private interests or are deemed to be 'luxuries' are not financed from health insurance. The list of these services is very long (twenty-four items), so it will not be listed here. Some examples are:

- medical tests not prescribed by a State physician;
- physical examinations for enrolment in schools, universities, etc., and other cases when the examination is not conducted strictly for the purpose of health protection;
- physical examinations and preventive measures conducted when sending persons to work abroad or on private trips;
- health protection associated with the treatment of acute alcoholism;
- termination of pregnancy for non-medical reasons;
- cosmetic surgical interventions (apart from those deemed necessary due to congenital malfunctions, functional disorders, severe injuries, etc.);
- hydrotherapy, hypnosis and the like;
- medical treatment of complications resulting from inadequate medical service, etc.[105]

132. Almost all insured persons are entitled to health protection that is financed from health insurance. Minor restrictions refer to, for example, foreign citizens,[106] certain dependants and some persons who are insured only against cases of occupational accidents and occupational diseases (*see* above). They are not entitled to free medical rehabilitation, prosthetics and auxiliary devices. However, they have access to these benefits as well if they fall under one of the following categories of persons exposed to greater risks of becoming ill: children, women in connection with pregnancy and maternity, persons older than 65 and persons suffering from serious diseases.

133. The scope, content and standards of health protection are determined by the Republic Fund for Health Insurance with the concurrence of the Government of the RS. The Fund has regulated this area through the Regulation on Conditions and Means of Acquiring Health Insurance Entitlements of 2 March 2010, and the Regulation on Content and Scope of Acquiring Health Protection from Obligatory Health

105. *See* Art. 110 of the Act on Health Insurance.

106. Among foreign nationals, the best financial position regarding health protection is enjoyed by nationals of the countries with which bilateral agreements on social insurance have been signed; foreigners who are in the country at the invitation of State institutions, asylum holders, victims of human trafficking, etc. *See* Arts 236–240 of the Act on Health Protection.

Insurance and Participation for 2019, of 6 February 2015.[107] Additionally, the Fund has established a so-called List of Medications that are Paid for By Health Insurance; conditions for receiving prosthetics, medical auxiliaries, dental prosthetic aids and supplies for their production; as well as conditions for medical rehabilitation services.[108]

134. In order to avoid excessive use of healthcare services, referrals are needed either from specialists or from medical committees for special health services such as laboratory tests, expensive scanning procedures, as well as for treatment at home and specialized rehabilitation.

135. There are no precise limitations regarding the type and amount of medications and health services that can be prescribed by physicians. There is only a principal agreement that medical workers have to apply only tested, safe, scientifically proven methods of treatment that have been certified in practice.[109]

136. In order to ensure conscientious and high-quality treatment, the law provides for a possibility of care control that can be conducted in several ways. First, there is internal and external supervision of the performance of health workers. Internal supervision is carried out by the head of the medical service or team, and major health institutions form expert boards, expert committees, ethics boards and committees responsible for improving quality of work.[110] For external supervision, the competent ministry appoints a prominent health worker, Fund or university to monitor the work. There are also professional bodies at State level: Health Council of Serbia, the Ethics Board and the National Expert Commissions, made up of prominent experts from the medical profession.[111] The second type of quality control can be instigated by the beneficiary who can submit a request for a second professional opinion, as well as a complaint concerning the quality and kind of health services provided. The complaint should be submitted to a special official, an ombudsman for patients' rights and to municipal Health Council.[112] The third type of quality control is conducted by health and pharmaceutical inspections; these are

107. Published in the Official Herald of the RS, Nos 10/2010, 18/2010, 46/2010, 52/2010, 80/2010, 60/2011; 1/2013, 108/2017; and Official Herald of the RS, No. 7/2019. The above-mentioned Regulation on Content and Scope of Acquiring Health Protection is being innovated each year.
108. *See* Regulation on the List of Prescription Medications to Be Issued at the Cost of Health Insurance (Official Herald of the RS, Nos 45/2018, 52/2018, 63/2018, 90/2018, 5/2019, 14/2019). Similar to other regulations as mentioned in this text previously, these acts are being innovated each year (some of them even few times a year).
109. The assessment is carried out by the National Institute for Public Health. *See* Art. 49 of the Act on Health Protection.
110. *See* Arts 126–143, and 187–196 of the Act on Health Protection.
111. *See* Arts 135–143 of the Act on Health Protection.
112. Since 2013, these functions were performed by an ombudsman for health care. The obdusman existed in every larger health institution from 2002. Today, these issues are regulated by a separate Act, i.e., the Act on Patients Rights of 2013 (*See* Arts 39–43).

charged with examining the legal side of the work of the health protection institution and assuring the proper functioning of medical equipment and drugs.[113] However, it should be mentioned that quality controls are often done superficially, which has led to a serious decline in the quality of healthcare. This, in turn, has produced a growing number of proceedings against physicians for malpractice.

§2. Amount of Benefit

137. The primary purpose of health insurance in Serbia is to secure financing for health protection costs (the second goal is to secure material benefits for the insured during their period of disability). In contrast to Western European countries, in Serbia, as well as in most former socialist countries, the reimbursement system is hardly ever applied (whereby the beneficiary first covers the cost of care himself/herself and is later refunded). Rather, the health insurance fund pays the healthcare institutions directly for services provided, which is why most health services are free of charge to the insured. This policy of free healthcare used to be emphasized as one of the greatest virtues of the social security system of the former socialist countries.[114]Since this kind of financing does not encourage a rational use of services, during the 1970s overconsumption of health services and hoarding of drugs, widely known as 'home pharmacies', was rampant. Consequently, the sharing of healthcare costs (i.e., co-payment) by the insured was introduced, especially in the areas where overconsumption was particularly obvious (in Serbia the sharing of costs is called 'participation'). A considerable effort was made to keep the co-payment at an acceptable level so that the poor would not be turned away from receiving healthcare services. Something similar is stipulated in Article 133, paragraph 2 of the Act on Health Insurance in Serbia. It is stipulated that the Health Care Minister establishes the maximum annual limit of participation for a particular healthcare service, taking into account that such participation does not prevent insured persons from using healthcare services, that is, to make it impossible for them to enjoy healthcare services to the full. This is particularly noticeable with more expensive medical procedures or examinations for which there are not enough financial resources from the health insurance fund due to the chronic financial crisis. Consequently, people on a low income who lack sufficient financial resources to cover the cost of the co-payment for appropriate diagnostic and medical procedures often do not receive adequate medical treatment.

138. The Act on Health Insurance determines precisely health services for which there may or may not be a co-payment. Basically, under Article 131 of the Act on Health Insurance, basic and most important forms of health protection to the amount of 65%–100% are covered by health insurance. Determining the specific amount of co-payment in health protection costs that should be charged is the duty of the

113. *See* Arts 246–250 of the Act on Health Protection.

114. *See* more about these characteristics of former socialist countries in: World Labour Report 2000, Income, Security and Social Protection in a Changing World (International Labour Office, 2000), 137.

Republic Fund for Health Insurance. Regulation on Content and Scope of Acquiring Health Protection from Obligatory Health Insurance and Participation in 2019 stipulates that a co-payment should be charged in cash amount or percentage of the cost of services or medication.

139. Participation in healthcare costs is established either on a flat-rate basis or as a percentage of the cost of services in accordance with the table contained in the Regulation (Article 2). Flat-rate amounts are usually set for standard health services and medication and are relatively low – they vary on a scale of RSD 50–RSD 900 (around EUR 0.42–EUR 7.6), but can reach up to RSD 30,000 (around EUR 250) in case of surgeries. Co-payment by way of a percentage of the total cost (between 5% and 100%) applies to non-standard healthcare services; more expensive and more complicated medical and diagnostic procedures; procurement of prosthetic, orthopaedic and other medical auxiliaries; as well as cosmetic medical procedures (*see* above). For hospital treatment, the amount of co-payment is symbolic – RSD 50 (around EUR 0.42) per day – and does not come close to covering real expenses.

140. In order to protect certain categories of individuals, many of them are exempted from the obligation to participate in the costs of many healthcare services (Article 37 of the Act on Health Insurance).[115] This includes all persons who enjoy free health protection as persons belonging to groups considered to be more exposed to health hazards with health protection for the treatment of the most frequent and difficult diseases (*see* above), as well as:

- war military invalids, non-war military invalids and civil war invalids;
- blind and permanently disabled persons, as well as persons receiving allowances for home care and assistance, in accordance with the regulations on pension and disability insurance (*see* further);
- voluntary blood donors, if they have donated blood ten times or more (or less, in the period of twelve months);
- voluntary blood donors, if they have donated blood less than ten times (with certain restrictions after twelve-month period from last blood donation);
- living organ donors;[116]
- cell and tissue donors;[117]
- children up to 18 years of age (and until the end of their education process – 26 years);
- persons involved in family planning and up to twelve months after giving birth;
- persons older than 65;
- unemployed persons (low-income persons);
- users of public dole whose foster person is serving in military;

115. Except in cases of obtaining mobile orthopaedic devices, cosmetic corrective procedures, drugs obtained abroad, and drugs, and services and medical supplies in connection with receiving health care treatment abroad. For cosmetic corrections of organs and body parts for military and non-military war invalids, whose injuries were caused by military actions after 17 Aug. 1990, no co-payment is required.

116. Certain medicines and medical equipment have been exempt from this category.

117. Certain medicines and medical equipment have been exempt from this category.

– persons of Romany nationality without permanent dwelling; and
– refugees and uprooted persons.

141. Generally, in this segment of the social security system, the principle of solidarity still figures very prominently. No limits regarding healthcare costs have been stipulated, regardless of the duration or total cost of treatment. An exception is stipulated under Article 52, paragraph 3 of the Act on Health Insurance, which makes provisions for the government to set certain priorities regarding health protection rights in cases of lack of funds or special circumstances.[118] In practical terms, the absence of limits regarding healthcare duration or cost has been an important guarantee of social security to families for years, considering that it is well-known how the costs of treatment can be a heavy burden for the budget of families with chronically ill members. However, in the last few years, this kind of security has been seriously tarnished due to the fact that many drugs cannot be found in State pharmacies where they could be obtained without paying, that is, where they are paid for by insurance. Consequently, many chronically ill patients, most of them elderly, have to purchase costly medication in private pharmacies. It is not uncommon for pensioners to have to allocate over 50% of their monthly income for medication, leaving many of them to survive at subsistence level (at the end of 2018, it was estimated that approximately 50% of the pensioners can be regarded as poor).[119] In addition, due to the recent lack of resources, it is not rare for insured persons to have to obtain and cover the costs of more expensive medical supplies, prostheses or medication, which cannot be found in State health institutions, hospitals or pharmacies, on their own. That amount is most often refunded, but only after months of delay. In these situations, the justifications for obtaining medication and supplies have to be especially verified by the Fund for Health Insurance (conducted by a special internal medical committee). The verification procedure, for which one often has to wait several months, is followed by an even longer delay in reimbursement.[120]

§3. Determining Rates of Fees and Prices

142. The practice of determining the prices of healthcare services in Serbia is an administrative task. The prices of healthcare services are set by the State (i.e., by the institutions for health insurance acting under State authority), allowing very little influence by the medical staff and the beneficiaries. The main reason for this

118. There is also financing of medical treatment for rare diseases from national budget contributions (paras 4 and 5).

119. *See Kako izgleda stariti u Srbiji: Polovina penzionera siromašna, odriču se svega da bi pomogli decu i unuke* (*What Ageing Looks Like in Serbia: Half of the Pensioners Are Poor, They Give up Everything to Support Their Children and Grandchildren*), 'Kurir' (daily newspaper), 9 September 2018, https://www.kurir.rs/vesti/drustvo/3117673/kako-izgleda-stariti-u-srbiji-polovina-penzionera-siromasna-odricu-se-svega-da-bi-pomogli-decu-i-unuke.

120. These kinds of costs, which the insured persons in the beginning have to cover themselves, can, for some illnesses (like cancer), reach an amount equal to tens or hundreds of times greater than the average pension or salary, that is, the price of a small apartment.

is the fact that most healthcare institutions are still in the hands of the State. Private practices and private hospitals are still fairly new and not widely accepted, although they are becoming more and more widespread. Private dental practices and pharmacies are more common due to the fact that the process of privatization for these sectors began in the 1990s. When it comes to the costs of treatment and the procurement of medication, the prices are predominantly determined by physicians, dentists and pharmacists (only the prices of some drugs are limited) and not by the State. State healthcare insurance does not normally finance these kinds of services or medical supplies, except possibly for a small amount for glasses, orthopaedic aids and deficit drugs, if these items cannot be obtained in State institutions and stores. In other words, if patients opt for medical treatment outside the State sector, they have to bear the costs themselves. However, due to sometimes protracted wait for medical services, a possibility to reimburse expenses for medical treatments received at privately owned medical institutions has been introduced. According to Regulation on Conditions and Means of Acquiring Health Insurance Entitlements of 2010, Articles 68 and 69, if medical treatments cannot be provided by state healthcare institutions within the course of thirty days (medical examination and medical rehabilitation) the insured can receive them at private healthcare institutions. They are obliged to pay for the medical service but are entitled to receive reimbursement for the expenses.[121]

143. Although Article 145 of the Health Protection and Article 197 of the Act on Health Insurance stipulates that the relationship between the Republic Fund for Health Insurance and other healthcare institutions should be regulated by periodical contracts, in reality only one contracted party (the Fund) has an influence on determining the fees for healthcare services. In practice, according to the Act on Health Insurance (Article 196), the Fund is authorized, with the consent of the Ministry, to determine conditions, criteria and rates, which are to govern contracting with some healthcare institutions.[122] In addition, the Fund is obligated to establish a 'nomenclature of healthcare services' (a list of healthcare services that are covered by health insurance) and other criteria for determining healthcare service fees.

144. The contract with healthcare institutions particularly determines: the types, scope and quality of healthcare services; the cost to the Fund for services rendered; the method of settling accounts and making payments; the method of resolving contentious issues; and other rights of the contracting parties (Article 197, paragraph 4 of the Act on Health Insurance). Concrete payments to the healthcare institution are determined according to individual services rendered, but payment per insured person can also be contracted. For those healthcare institutions with which no contract exists, the Fund pays only for services rendered in cases of emergency.[123]

---

121. *See* Republički fond za zdravstveno osiguranje, Refundacija, https://rfzo.rs/index.php/osiguranalica/refundacija.
122. *See* Regulation on Conditions, Criteria and Rates for Contracting with Some Health Care Institutions and Paying Institutions in 2015, of 28 Dec. 2019 (Official Herald of the RS, No. 8/2019). These regulations are being innovated each year i.e., a new regulation is being brought each year.
123. *See* Art. 205 of the Act on Health Insurance.

145. Contracts with healthcare institutions are to be signed by the branch offices of the Fund in their respective districts. Prices for providing healthcare services that are financed from the national budget and not from contributions are determined in a similar way. Healthcare institutions are entitled to an allowance for the services rendered, which includes financial resources for:

- the payment of salaries and other means of income to employees who provide healthcare services;
- the costs of drugs from the 'List of Medications Issued at the Expense of the Insurance' and other approved medical supplies used during treatment.[124]

At least once every six months, the healthcare institutions submit their invoices to the branch offices of the Fund for their services, in accordance with the prices from the current list of Fees for Health Care Services in Health Care Institutions of the RS.[125] The fees from the price list are adjusted periodically (once a year, or every other year) to reflect changes in the cost of living.

146. The above-mentioned methods of determining prices of healthcare services apply uniformly to all types of healthcare institutions. Certain minor differences that might appear when contracting fees with individual institutions are purely of a technical nature.[126]

147. In practice, contracts for providing healthcare services are almost exclusively signed with State healthcare institutions (which are in the Plan of Health Institutions Network). In Article 70 of the above-mentioned Regulation on Conditions, Criteria and Rates for Contracting with Some Health Care Institutions and Paying Institutions, provisions have been made for contracts to be signed with private institutions as well (with those which are not included in the Plan of Network of Health Care Institutions), if it is necessary to engage additional healthcare assets in order to meet the needs of the insured persons for particular kinds of medical services which are included in/covered by compulsory health insurance.

§4. Budget Limitation

148. Over the years, the healthcare branch has suffered from progressively deeper deficits because the State has never formally placed any budgetary limits on expenditures. However, in reality this limit was manifested by the complete lack of

124. *See* above-mentioned Regulation on the List of Medications Issued at the Expense of the Insurance, of 2018 (Official Herald of the RS, Nos 45/2018, 52/2018, 63/2018, 90/2018, 5/2019, 14/2019).
125. *See* Art. 85 of the Regulation on Conditions, Criteria and Rates for Contracting with Some Health Care Institutions and Paying Institutions.
126. Special provisions have been made for contracting services with pharmacies, pharmaceutical institutions, bureaus and institutions for the protection of health, institutions for special medical rehabilitation, institutions of social protection, orthopaedic companies and stores, and opticians.

financial resources, which further caused a systematic decrease in the State's financing of health protection each year. This is the reason behind the drastic decline in the quality of healthcare services and the quality of equipment and appliances, and a chronic deficit in medical supplies and medication. However, it was impossible to increase co-payments for costs of health protection because of the progressively lower incomes within the overall population.

149. In addition, no specialized body that would, in the tradition of some European countries, supervise rational spending of health insurance resources in the name of the society has been established as of yet.[127] Control of expenditure is under the jurisdiction of the Ministry of Health.[128]

---

127. *See* J. van Langendonck, *Belgium*, in *International Encyclopaedia of Laws, Social Security Law* (Prof. Dr R. Blanpain (gen. ed.), W. van Eeckhoutte & M. van Opstal (ed.)), 83.
128. *See* http://www.zdravlje.gov.rs.

Chapter 3. Conditions

150. In order to be able to exercise one's health insurance rights, every insured person must be affiliated with an authorized branch office of the Republic Fund for Health Insurance. Another condition to exercising one's health insurance rights (and for rights of family members) is that the health contributions have been made, and that the person has had three months' continuous insurance or a six-month insurance with intervals over the last eighteen months. The exemptions are persons who have suffered an occupational injury or occupational disease, in cases of medical emergencies, and persons entitled to cash benefits due to incapacity to work – to the amount of a minimum wage.[129]

151. The responsible branch office for each insured person is determined either by his/her place of work or by place of residence. The branch office keeps a file on each registered person and a record of all matters in connection with health insurance entitlements for each beneficiary.[130] The application for insurance that should be submitted is as follows:

- for wage earners, their family members, as well as for themselves and their families – by the employer, that is, the company or institution in which the wage earner is employed;
- for pension beneficiaries or persons exercising other rights from that insurance branch, as well as for their family members – by the Pension and Disability Insurance Institution;
- for unemployed persons and their family members – by the Employment Fund.

152. The application form has to be submitted before signing/within eight days after signing an employment contract or not later than the day after starting work.[131] The same deadline applies for reporting any changes to or the cancellation of the insurance. If the employer fails to submit the application, the interested party can personally file a request to the Republic Fund for Health Insurance to be recognized as an insured person.[132]

153. Once the application has been submitted, the branch office of the Fund issues a document confirming a person's status as a registered insured person, which is called a health card.[133] An insured person can enjoy free healthcare services only with a validated health card.[134] In mid-2017 *automated health card certification* was introduced and since then health cards held by the employed and most other social

129. *See* Art. 50 of the Act on Health Insurance.
130. About registration of the insured, keeping records and other details that are covered in this section, *see* further in the Act on Health Insurance (Arts 24–48) and Arts 3–17 of the Regulation on Conditions and Means of Acquiring Health Insurance Entitlements.
131. *See* para. 2 of the Art. 35 of the Act on Labour and Art. 12 para. 2 of the Act on the Central Register of Compulsory Social Insurance.
132. *See* Art. 24 of the Act on Health Insurance.
133. *See* Arts 25 and 26 of the Act on Health Insurance.
134. *See* Art. 26 of the Act on Health Insurance.

categories have been automatically validated (using the data provided by the Central Register of Social Insurance).[135] For the insured in independent professions, farmers and their family members, persons under 18 years of age as well as pupils and students, automated certification is not available and their health cards have to be validated at the Republic Health Insurance Fund branch offices.

154. As a rule, healthcare services are provided in healthcare institutions that are located in the district of the branch offices where the beneficiaries have been insured.[136] Only for emergencies and in special cases can services be provided in an institution located outside of this territory. Most healthcare services are performed by a general practitioner. When services are not performed by a general practitioner, he/she has to fill out referrals to be seen by a specialist. Some special healthcare services can be prescribed only by a specialist or a medical committee.

155. As previously mentioned, certain and mainly the more expensive health services and auxiliaries, which fall outside the scope of standard services (e.g., the need for treatment at home, specialized rehabilitation), and treatment abroad, have to be approved by special medical committees that operate within the system of the Fund branch office. The medical advisors on these committees are independent of the Fund because they are not employed by it, but perform these duties as part-time external advisors.

156. The law does not contain particular provisions regarding grounds for exclusion of healthcare services. These grounds are indirectly covered by legal provisions on damage compensation, which contain regulations on cases that allow the Fund to request restitution for expenses for healthcare services (as well as for benefits during incapacity to work) from the insured. In short, persons are obliged to pay compensation for costs to the Fund if they have been enjoying benefits based on incorrect information or of a higher amount than they are entitled to. The Fund is also entitled to compensation of the costs of healthcare from persons who have caused the illness, injury or death of the insured. This type of compensation can also be requested from the employer if another worker caused the illness or injury or if the company failed to properly implement work protection measures or other protective measures for employees. The Fund is also entitled to damage compensation from physicians or healthcare organizations for incorrect treatment and medical malpractice. Compensation for damage is also possible from the insurance company, if the healthcare costs were caused by a car accident.[137] This means that the serious fault of the insured persons themselves are not direct grounds for exclusion of healthcare, but it can be grounds for the exclusion of material benefits during their incapacity to work or reason for restitution of expenses for healthcare services.

---

135. *See Republički fond za zdravstveno osiguranje, Automatska overa zdravstvenih kartica (Republic Health Insurance Fund, Automated Health Card Certification),* https://www.rfzo.rs/index.php/vesti/973-automatska-overa-zk.
136. *See* Art. 124 of the Act on Health Insurance and Art. 17 of the Regulation on Conditions and Means of Acquiring Health Insurance Entitlements.
137. *See* Arts 218–227 of the Act on Health Insurance.

157. All compensation claims against the health insurance system must be made to the Fund within three years.[138] If the insured person is not satisfied with the decision by the Fund, he/she is entitled to initiate a trial within three years from the day of learning about the decision and five years from the day the incident causing the claim took place.[139] More precisely, two kinds of court trials are possible: (1) A trial against the Republic Health Insurance Fund and (2) a trial against a healthcare institution or medical worker (a doctor, nurse etc.). In the first case, according to Article 167 of the Act on Health Insurance, an administrative dispute trial can be initiated against the final decision made by the Republic Fund regarding a right guaranteed by compulsory health insurance. This kind of trial is held in the Administrative Court and against the Republic Health Insurance Fund if the insured think they have been deprived of a guaranteed right or that a particular right has been wrongly determined. In the other case, a patient can file a lawsuit to the Civil Court claiming compensation for the damages. According to Article 31 of the Act on Patients' Rights, of 22 May 2013, patients who have suffered damage to their bodies or whose medical condition has deteriorated due to professional mistakes or negligence by medical workers or medical staff are entitled to receive compensation according to general regulations regarding liability for the damage. According to Article 31, paragraph 2, the Act on Patients' Rights, the right to claim damages cannot be excluded or limited in advance (by signing a personal statement prior to medical treatment or surgery).

138. *See* Art. 109 para. 2 of the Act on Health Insurance.

139. With regard to these requests and deadlines, the same norms that apply to other obligations are appropriate here as well, as contained in the former federal, and now republic, Act on Contracts and Torts (Official Gazette of the SFRY, Nos 29/1978, 39/1985, 45/1989, 57/1989, and FRY Nos 31/1993, 22/99, 44/99, Official Herald of the RS, No. 1/2003).

Part IV. Family Allowances

158. Family allowances in Serbia are formally quite developed and diverse. The reason for this is that family allowances was an area that received great attention in the former Yugoslavia. Until the economic and political crisis of the 1990s, the rights to which children and families were entitled were among the most progressive in the world. As the economic crisis deepened, a severe decline gradually followed, which has been reflected in the dwindling amounts of family allowances, as well as in the timeliness of payments (for instance, by the end of the 1990s, child allowances were more than two years in arrears). The current system of family allowances is rather outdated given demographic and other trends and practices (reconciliation of work and family, family friendly schemes etc.). In 2017, by implementing a new Act on Financial Allowances for Families with Children, the Government made a moderately successful attempt to strengthen that system with the aim of encouraging an increase in birth rate The main advantage of this law is the extension of the list of people who are entitled to family allowances (the list now includes women entrepreneurs, female smallholding owners, women engaged in temporary and part-time jobs and unemployed women who had an income over the course of eighteen months prior to giving birth). Regarding some rights, however, there has been a step back and there are circumstances in which mothers receive less than EUR 10 as a compensation for maternity leave.[140]

159. The current system of family allowances in Serbia provides the following benefits: maternity benefits (maternity leave), child allowances, birth grants, compensation and reimbursement of costs for nurseries and preschool institutions, subsidizing rest and recreational activities for children, subsidizing students' meals, and so on. The positive side of this system is that all of these benefits are financed from the national budget and not on the basis of insurance. In other words, these rights are primarily conditioned on the needs of families and children rather than on the financial contributions and financial capabilities of the parents.

160. However, in the last few years, due to the many negative economic trends within the country, the economic status of families has drastically declined. This in

140. *See Novine, prednosti i mane novog Zakona o finansijskoj podršci porodici sa decom (News, Advantages and Disadvantages of the New Act on Financial Support to the Family with Children),* Unija, https://unija.com/novine-prednosti-i-mane-novog-zakona-o-finansijskoj-podrsci-porodici-sa-decom/?lang=sr.

turn has been reflected in a serious drop in the birth rate in Serbia.[141] Therefore, in order to stimulate the birth rate, the Act on Financial Aid to Families with Children was adopted on 5 April 2002, introducing entitlement incentives to families with many children.[142] However, this Act was not very successful so it was replaced by a new one in 2017 (*see* above).

141. Over the past twenty years, a negative birth rate (around 3%) has been recorded in Serbia. *See* G. Nikolić, *Zablude o opasnostima usled negativnog prirodnog priraśstaja u Srbiji (Prejudices about Negative Birth-Rate Consequences in Serbia)*, B92, 2007, http://blog.b92.net/text/697/Zablude-o-opasnostima-usled-negativnog-prirodnog-prirastaja-u-Srbiji/. *See also: Alarmatno: U samo šest opština u Srbiji pozitivan prirodni priraštaj! (Alarming: Only Six Municipalities in Serbia Have a Positive Birth Rate Increase!)*, 'Kurir', (daily press), 6 Nov. 2018, https://www.kurir.rs/vesti/drustvo/3150127/alarmantno-u-samo-sest-opstina-u-srbiji-pozitivan-prirodni-prirastaj.

142. The Act was published in the Official Herald of the RS, Nos 16/2002, 115/2005, 107/2009. Also, the old law that used to govern this area – the Act on Social Care for Children of 21 Jul. 1992, still applies partially to some family allowance benefits in Serbia. Published in the Official Herald of the RS, Nos 49/1992, 29/1993, 53/1993, 53/1993, 67/1993, 67/1993, 28/1994, 47/1994, 48/1994, 25/1996, 29/2001, 16/2002, 62/2003, 101/2005, 18/2010.

Chapter 1. Field of Application

§1. Territorial Field of Application

161. In Serbia, the territorial field of application for family allowances is primarily conditioned on the place of residence of the parents, although this is not explicitly stipulated (except in the case of birth grant and child allowances).[143] As far as the child is concerned, it is assumed that he/she lives with the parents because one of the requests is for the parents to be primary caretakers. Regarding child allowances, it is also required that the child receives his/her education in the country and to attend school regularly.[144] Regarding maternity benefits, from the Act on Financial Aid to Families with Children, Article 12, it could be concluded that the parent is expected either to work with a domestic employer or to be self-employed within the territory of the country. As an exception, persons working for a limited time abroad are also entitled to this benefit.

162. A child spending time abroad is not considered a hindrance to receiving family allowances, but it follows from the requirements in the Act on Financial Aid to Families with Children that these periods abroad may be only short-term (e.g., shorter stays for tourist purposes or for the benefit of the child's health). In other words, the parent should be the immediate caretaker of the child, while living or working in Serbia.

§2. Personal Field of Application

163. The personal field of application of family allowances is basically very broad. The intention of the legislators was to make benefits available to a circle of beneficiaries as large as possible. However, due to limited resources, certain rights have been conditioned by a number of requirements based mainly on social criteria, thereby reducing the prospective number of beneficiaries.

164. Mostly, it is one parent, primarily the mother, who exercises the right to financial benefits. This is true of maternity benefits, child allowances and birth grants, while certain rights are intended for the children directly (such as compensation or reimbursement for the costs of preschool and nurseries).

165. For most benefits, except maternity leave, the entitlement to family allowances is not based on whether or not the parent is employed, because the whole system is financed from the republic budget (only resources for reimbursements for nursery costs are provided by the local municipality or the city).

166. The basic condition for entitlement to any of these benefits is that the parent is the primary caretaker of the child. This is why the father can take advantage

143. Articles 22 and 26 of the Act on Financial Aid to Families with Children.
144. *See* Arts 24 and 26 of the Act on Financial Aid to Families with Children.

of most family allowance benefits as well, if the mother is for some reason unable, and if she is unavailable, it applies to the guardian or the foster or adoptive parent.[145] If the parent fails to care for the child in a manner deemed appropriate, the child may be placed in the care of a third party, in which case the third party is entitled to these benefits.

167. The next important condition (which is actually an issue only in connection with child and birth grants) is domestic citizenship of the parent. Foreign nationals working on the territory of the RS are entitled to child allowances and that right is granted to mothers who are foreign citizens and have a status of permanently settled foreigners (regarding birth grant, a child has to be born in the territory of the RS).[146] Regarding maternity benefits, nationality is not mentioned as an obstacle to exercise this right.

---

145. This is explicitly stipulated regarding maternity benefits, other benefits and child allowances. Arts 12, 17, 26 of the Act on Financial Aid to Families with Children.
146. *See* Arts 22 para. 2 and 26 of the Act on Financial Aid to Families with Children.

Chapter 2. Dependent Children

168. In order to become entitled to family allowance, in addition to the parents complying with the requirements, the child must also satisfy several conditions. First, a link has to be established between the child and the beneficiary. As a rule, it should be a member of the immediate family, that is, the link should be between a parent and a child. For certain other rights, the term 'family' has a broader meaning, comprised of entitlements by horizontal kinship, that is, siblings, and children of the spouse/partner. As previously mentioned, an important factor in certain cases can be whether or not the children live under the same roof as the parent, that is, whether the parent is the primary caretaker (this applies to maternity leave, other benefits, birth grants and child allowance).

169. Second, the age of the child is an important factor. Certain rights are conditioned by age-limits, such as:

- the right to paid maternity leave (maternity benefit or parental grant) is provided after the birth of the child;[147]
- the right to paid leave to care for a child – this is a benefit used after maternity leave, starting with the child's third month (a total duration of 365 days starting with the first day of maternity leave; the paid leave is two years for the third and each following child);
- if the child is adopted or has a legal guardian – the leave to care for the child may be used until the age of 5, for a duration of eight to eleven months (depending on the child's age);
- the right to leave from work or part-time work to provide special care for the child may be used until the age of 5;
- child allowance may normally be used until the age of 21 and not longer than the age of 26 with extended parental guardianship;
- the right to attend kindergarten may, as a rule, be used as long as it is attended which is usually until the age of 7;
- the right to rest and recreation in children's recreation centres may be used until the age of 15.[148]

170. Other conditions prescribed for certain benefits depend generally on the number of children, the overall health of the child and the family's economic status.[149]

147. Maternity leave starts at the earliest forty-five days and at the latest twenty-eight days prior to giving birth, and lasts up to three months after the delivery date.
148. The cited rights are regulated by Art. 11 of the Act on Financial Aid to Families with Children, Arts 89–99 of the Act on Labour and Arts 33 and 34 of the Act on Social Care for Children.
149. For example, child allowance will be granted to those whose total income does not exceed the amount of two average incomes per family head. *See* Art. 7 of the Act on Financial Aid to Families with Children and at the link of the Ministry: https://www.minrzs.gov.rs/sr/node/181189. *See also*: Regulation on Particular Conditions and Means to Attain the Rights to Financial Aid for Families with Children.

Chapter 3. Amount of the Benefit

171. The family allowance amounts in Serbia are primarily dependent on the social status of the parents and the number of children. The issue of financial contributions is taken into account only with regard to the maternity benefit, for which it is important whether the individual is a wage earner or self-employed, as well as the length of his/her contribution period. The amounts are calculated per month and balanced against the cost of living.

§1. Maternity Benefit

172. Maternity benefit is provided in the amount equalling the average basic salary the person realized over an eighteen-month period preceding the leave from work.[150]

173. In addition to maternity benefit the employed have the right to additional benefits regarding birth, childcare and special childcare which are available to new mothers in the same amount as for employed women under the following conditions:

(1) if she is unemployed at the time of giving birth and has not realized the right to receive financial aid granted to the unemployed;
(2) if she is self-employed;
(3) if she is an owner of a family smallholding with the same status as a self-employed person;
(4) if she has a temporary and/or part-time job contract;
(5) if she has a temporary (civil) service contract;
(6) if she has a copyright contract;
(7) on the basis of the contract regarding the rights and duties of managers who are outside employment.[151]

174. A lower and an upper limit have been determined for this right – the threshold equals the minimum income for the month in which payments are made, and the highest amount cannot go above three times the average salary in the Republic.[152]

150. Article 108 of the Act on Labour anticipates a wage increase of 0.4% for each year of work for the same employer.
151. *See* Art. 17 of the Act on Financial Aid to Families with Children.
152. *See* Arts 13 and 18 of the Act on Financial Aid to Families with Children.

§2. Compensation in Case of Absence from Work or Part-Time Work Due to Special Childcare Benefit

175. This entitlement applies to one parent or to the guardian of such children who need special care due to serious psychological and/or physical disabilities, and may be used after the end of maternity leave. The amount equals the amount of maternity leave compensation, or in proportion to the hours worked for part-time employees.[153]

§3. Birth Grant

176. The right to birth grant was introduced in Serbia in 2002, with the goal of stimulating the birth rate. It is granted to mothers for their first, second, third and fourth child if they are the primary caretakers of the child. The father may also take advantage if the mother has passed away or is prevented from caring for the child. The amounts of compensation were increased by the new law of 2017 and are currently fixed at:

- for the first child, RSD 99,800.00 (about EUR 845);
- for the second child, RSD 239,520.00 (about EUR 2,029);[154]
- for the third child, RSD 1,437,120.00 (about EUR 12,178);[155]
- for the fourth child, RSD 2,155,680.00 (about EUR 18,268).[156]

The amount of compensation for the first child is paid in full. For each following child, it is paid in equal monthly instalments. The amounts are regularly (twice a year) adjusted for the cost of living.[157]

§4. Child Allowance

177. In Serbia, only underprivileged persons are entitled to a child allowance, not all insured parents, as is the case in some European countries.

---

153. This right is envisaged in Art. 96, para. 4 of the Act on Labour. The conditions for exercising this right are stipulated in Arts 2–19 of the Regulation on Particular Conditions and Means to Attain the Rights to Financial Aid for Families with Children (*see* above).
154. It is paid in equal monthly instalments over the period of twenty-four months – monthly rate amounts to: RSD 9,980 (about EUR 85).
155. It is paid over the period of ten years, a monthly rate amounts to: RSD 11,976 (about EUR 101).
156. It is paid over the period of ten years, a monthly rate amounts to: RSD 17,964.00 (about EUR 152). These are the amounts for June, 2019, *see* https://www.paragraf.rs/statistika/nominalni_iznosi_prava_na_finansijsku_podrsku_porodici_sa_decom_i_cenzusi_za_ostvarivanje_prava_na_deciji_dodatak.html.
157. The amounts for childcare benefits, *see*: http://www.minrzs.gov.rs/cir/visine-socijalnih-davanja.

178. Receiving child allowances is conditioned on the fact that income per family head does not exceed a certain amount (which is occasionally adjusted according to the cost of living index).[158] Compensation is due for the first four children and is determined from an index-linked fixed amount.[159] Objectively, the amount in question is very low, starting at RSD 2,994.00 (about EUR 25). For single parents, foster parents and legal guardians the compensation amount is increased by 30% (RSD 3,892.20 to about EUR 33). For parents of children with developmental difficulties and parents of children with disabilities, child allowance is increased by 50%. Child allowance recipients whose children have regularly attended secondary school and finished the school year with merits are entitled to additional monthly child allowance in September of that current year.[160]

§5. Other Benefits

179. Compensation for the costs of attending day care for children without parental care and children with disabilities is paid in an amount that equals the service's fees. Regarding the right to reimbursement for attending day care for children from underprivileged families, as well as the right to rest and recreation for children up to 15 years of age, the method and conditions for reimbursement are determined by the municipal or city administration, since they are the organs financing these rights. Article 35 of the Act on Social Care for Children, of 21 July 1992 (previously the governing Act in this area, nowadays applied only to a certain extent) stipulates that reimbursement can cover not more than 80% of the market price of day care this way. Besides, the city or municipality as well as the Autonomous Province may decide to allocate additional reimbursement or to increase the existing amount of reimbursement. This was, for example, initially done by the

158. For example, child allowance will be granted to those whose total income does not exceed the amount of two average incomes per employed (in the Republic of Serbia) without taxes and contributions per family head. As well as that, the right to child allowance can be obtained if an applicant or his/her family members do not own any property either in the Republic of Serbia or abroad apart from the housing where the family lives, which cannot be larger than one bedroom per household member plus one additional room. *See* Arts 7 and 8 of the Act on Financial Aid to Families with Children and at the link of the Ministry: https://www.minrzs.gov.rs/sr/node/181189. Also *see*: Regulation on Particular Conditions and Means to Attain the Rights to Financial Aid for Families with Children.

159. Exceptionally, foster-parent or tutor can receive child allowance for maximum four children of his/her own and for each foster-child. *See* Art. 26, para. 5 of the Act on Financial Aid to Families with Children.

160. *See* Art. 33 of the Act on Financial Aid to Families with Children.

Autonomous Province (when it increased the birth grant amount for the first child covering it from its own funds),[161] and thereafter followed by some other big cities as well.[162]

161. This right does not exist anymore but the Province Government introduced the right to 'maternal allowance' in 2018 which refers to unemployed mothers with three or four children. Since January 2019 the amount paid to those entitled to this right has been RSD 15,000 (approx. EUR 127). *See* Provincial Decision to Provide Material Allowance for Unemployed Mothers for Third or Fourth Children (The Official Gazette of the Autonomous Province of Vojvodina, 60/2018) and Executive Order Related to Parent's Entitlement for the First Child (The Official Gazette of the Autonomous Province of Vojvodina, No. 13/2005).
162. *See* Executive Order to the Right to Financial Allowances to Families with Children (The Official Gazette of the City of Novi Sad, Nos 30/2010, 45/2010, 10/2012).

Chapter 4. Payment

180. All family allowances provided by the Republic (and by the Autonomous Province Vojvodina) are paid for by the city/municipal administration. Only maternity benefit is paid by the Ministry of labour, employment, war veterans and social affairs. As a rule, territorial competence pertains to bodies in the locality of the place of residence of the beneficiary. Appeals to decisions by first-degree bodies are handled by the minister for social affairs (in the Autonomous Province of Vojvodina, it is the appropriate provincial secretariat – the Provincial Department for Health, Social Policy, Demography.[163] Regarding entitlements under the competence of the city/municipality, their administration determines which bodies are to implement the execution of these rights. Most often this falls under the jurisdiction of the bodies that are responsible for other family allowances.

163. *See* http://www.vojvodina.gov.rs/sr/секретаријати/пс-за-здравство-социјалну-политику-и-демографију?page=1.

Part V. Incapacity to Work

Chapter 1. Field of Application

181. As mentioned previously, the Serbian health insurance covers two different social risks simultaneously: the need for healthcare and the need for cash benefits during the period of disability. The reason for this is that these risks intertwine regarding the population able to work, since they are caused by the same source – illness or injury. Both risks are administered by the same institution – the Republic Fund for Health Insurance. There are certain departments within these institutions that specialize in conducting the administrative work in connection with each of these risks.

§1. Territorial Field of Application

182. Regarding the territorial field of application, the conditions for entitlement to cash benefits are the same as those concerning healthcare (*see* above). Considering that these two segments of social security are connected, they are also regulated by the same laws and, to a great extent, uniformly. As a rule, compensation based on health insurance is paid to insured persons who reside and work in the country. As an exception, compensation can also be received by insured persons working on a limited assignment abroad for a local firm and also by citizens of Serbia working abroad (*see* above).

§2. Personal Field of Application

183. The personal field of application is not the same for all cash benefits as it is for the obligation to contribute. As a rule, it is slightly narrower regarding all benefits, except regarding compensation for transportation costs. Only employed domestic citizens and self-employed persons (including priests and other religious workers; public notaries and bailiffs) are entitled to cash benefits in the case of temporary incapacity to work. Since 2019 farmers and other agricultural workers are also entitled to this right.[164]

164. *See* Art. 72 of the Act on Health Insurance.

Chapter 2. Kinds of Benefits

184. The cash benefits within the health insurance system in Serbia cover the following risks:

- short- and medium-term incapacity to work due to illness or accident (cash benefit);
- transportation costs associated with obtaining health coverage (cash benefits).

185. The maternity risk, which in some countries belongs to this branch, is not financed by health insurance in Serbia, but by family allowances (this branch is financed from the national budget).

§1. Incapacity to Work

186. In addition to sickness and injury, incapacity to work is the most important risk covered by health insurance in Serbia. The concept of incapacity to work is basically the same for wage earners, public-sector employees and self-employed persons (there is only a minor difference for the last group). The compensation for incapacity to work that is covered by health insurance is widely known as 'sickness benefit'.

I. Wage Earners

187. There is no strict legal definition for incapacity to work. From a legal and normative context, it could be perceived as a temporary (short- and medium-term) incapacity or inability to perform one's work due to health reasons.[165] In Article 81 of the Act on Health Insurance, it is stipulated that in case of a long-term state of incapacity to work (six months) or a twelve-month incapacity over the past eighteen months, the insured person has to be directed to the Health Committee for assessment of his/her loss of ability to work.[166]

188. However, the Act on Health Insurance in Article 73 provides a precise list of cases of temporary incapacity that are covered by health insurance. These are:

- if the temporary incapacity to work is due to illness or injury;
- if the person is unable to work due to a high-risk pregnancy;

165. *See* Art. 76 of the Act on Health Insurance,
166. According to para. 1 Art. 80 of the Act on Health Insurance, a physician i.e., the Medical Commission shall, irrespective of the duration and the cause of temporary incapacity for work, direct the insured person for further assessment by the competent Body should their finding indicate that the health condition of the insured person demonstrates the loss of working capacity.

- if the person has been identified as a germ carrier and placed in isolation for that reason, or because of an outbreak of an infectious disease in his/her immediate surroundings;
- if the person has been assigned to nurse a sick member of his/her immediate family in compliance with the conditions stipulated in this Act;
- if the person has been incapacitated by undergoing voluntary organ or tissue donor transplant surgery (voluntary donation of organs and tissues), excluding voluntary blood donation;
- if the person has been assigned to escort a sick person referred to another city for treatment or for a medical examination.

189. Evidently, sickness and injury of the insured are not the only risks covered by this insurance – it also covers pregnancy or organ donor procedures, as well as sickness or injury of a person close to the insured person.

190. Although the law does not specify this issue, in order to become entitled to sick leave, a person must, for health reasons, be unable to perform the job that is his/her current occupation; it does not apply to some other work that the person may be capable of performing. A person's health status prior to employment is not taken into account because labour legislation indirectly stipulates that a person cannot enter into an employment contract unless he/she is capable of performing the relevant job (except in the case of handicapped persons, who can be trained for employment specifically designed to meet their special needs) – *see* further.

191. While receiving the 'sickness benefit' employed persons (or self-employed persons) are not allowed to perform any activities that would generate income. The one exception to this rule refers only to wage earners: if it is determined during their treatment that their overall health has improved to such an extent that partial work would be of further benefit, it can be arranged for them to work only part-time – not less than four hours per day – for a limited period of time. These hours cannot be maintained for longer than three months in continuation or with discontinuities over the period of twelve months.[167]

192. If during the period of incapacity to work, the beneficiary engages in commercial or other profitable activities, he/she loses the right to salary compensation. According to labour law, this constitutes a misuse of the sickness benefit and can be the grounds for dismissal.[168]

II. The Self-Employed

193. For wage earners in Serbia, the concept of incapacity to work also pertains to self-employed persons, with the reservation that some segments of the concept are adapted to the specificities of self-employed persons. According to Article 85 of

167. *See* Art. 99 of the Act on Health Insurance.
168. *See* Art. 179 of the Act on Labour.

the Act on Health Insurance, the owner or founder of an enterprise is entitled to compensation during the period of incapacity to work only if he/she has previously announced the cancellation of business activities. However, if this person employs one or more workers, then he/she is allowed to maintain the enterprise in operation, but in this case, he/she is only entitled to half of the sickness benefit.

194. Therefore, the criterion for incapacity to work for the self-employed is the cessation of personal involvement in business activities. If the person employs workers, the business may be conducted with the help of these persons and may continue to generate income. This is a feasible solution because self-employed persons generally live on the premises where the work is carried out. It is therefore in everyone's interest to have occupational activity continued, at least at the level of minimal necessary tasks, in order to ensure continuity of business. Therefore, it is not logical that there are no provisions for the self-employed, as in the case of wage earners, to resume partial or light work with the permission of a medical adviser. Potential abuse of this right could be avoided by introducing high-quality assessment of the self-employed person's capacity to work and conducting regular control procedures.

§2. Travel Expenses Benefit

195. The insured person, his/her family members or appointed escorts to the sick person, if necessary, entitled to compensation for their travel costs connected with obtaining health protection.[169] The following conditions must be met:

- that a physician has referred, or invited, the insured person to a distant location, either for medical treatment or for an assessment of capacity to work by another physician;
- that the location of the treatment facility is at least 50 km from the insured person's place of residence;
- regardless of distance, if the person in question has been prescribed to undergo dialysis treatments, or if it is a child or disabled person whose treatment consists of therapy as prescribed by the medical committee (at least twice a week).[170]

196. If the insured person becomes sick outside of his/her place of work or place of residence, the person is not entitled to compensation for travel costs, except in the case that a special type of transportation is required.

197. Travel costs are calculated on the shortest possible route, in the price range equal to a second-class train or bus ticket. As an exception, if there is a specific

169. It is considered obligatory to appoint an escort to children under the age of 18 who require medical treatment, as well as to an elderly person with severe physical or mental disability or any other person unable to perform everyday activities on his/her own due to poor health. *See* Art. 107 of the Act on Health Insurance.

170. *See* Art. 103 of the Act on Health Insurance.

requirement for a certain type of transportation, such costs will also be covered. Persons who are entitled to ambulance transportation, but do not receive this service when needed, are entitled to compensation in the amount of the actual travel costs (up to an amount equal to 10% of the price of 1 litre fuel per km travelled). Also, persons who, due to the lack of public transportation, have to use their private vehicles for urgent or medically justifiable reasons, are entitled to this same type of compensation.[171]

171. *See* Art. 104 of the Act on Health Insurance.

Chapter 3. Certification of Incapacity to Work

198. The official recognition of the state of incapacity to work is the same for all insured persons, but those responsible for assessing this state differ, depending on the duration and cause of the incapacity.

Certification of incapacity to work is conducted in the following ways:

- in regular cases, for short-term incapacity, the assessment is made by general practitioners or specialists in occupational medicine;
- if the wage earner's child is sick – by a paediatrician;
- if the reason is pregnancy or other gynaecological problems – by a gynaecologist;
- if the incapacity to work lasts more than thirty days (or more than seven days in the case of nursing a member of the immediate family, and more than fifteen days in the case of caring for a child under 15 years of age) – by a medical committee from the local branch office of the Republic Fund for Health Insurance.[172]

199. After the examination, the wage earner receives a certification of his/her temporary incapacity to work. In addition to data about the health institution and about the wage earner, this certification also contains the following information:

- the starting date of the temporary incapacity to work;
- the grounds for the temporary incapacity to work;
- a diagnosis of the disease;
- the expected duration of the incapacity;
- the signature of the physician, with the official stamp of the health institute.[173]

200. At the same time, the physician writes all major information in connection with the incapacity to work in the employee's 'health file'. This file contains all medical records for the insured person and is kept within the person's primary healthcare institution.

201. In order to avoid abuse, provisions have been made for certain types of control measures when determining the state of incapacity to work. A physician should refer the insured person to a medical committee for certification of their incapacity to work in the following cases:

- if the insured person is unable to work for a total period exceeding thirty days;

---

172. *See* Arts 78 and 81 of the Act on Health Insurance.
173. The content of the certificate is regulated by Art. 3 of the Regulation on the Method of Issuing and Contents of the Certificate of Temporary Incapacity to Work of Wage Earners in Light of Health Insurance Regulation of 14 Jan. 2002, Official Herald or the RS, No. 1/2002. According to Act on Labour, Art. 103, para. 1: 'Any employee shall, not later than three days after the conditions for temporary inability to work have occurred, pursuant to health insurance regulations, furnish the appropriate medical certificate stating the expected duration of the temporary inability to work.'.

– if the insured person is unable to work for a total period of thirty days in a period of forty-five days, with intervals in between periods of their incapacity, due to a succession of illnesses.[174]

202. Furthermore, the employer has the right to initiate a re-assessment of the state of incapacity to work by the medical committee if there are doubts about the justification for the absence from work.[175] If the person in question fails to comply with the request for a re-examination without reasonable cause, compensation payments will be cancelled.

203. The law has provisions for yet another type of control measure for the determination of the state of incapacity to work. This pertains to cases when a long-term state of incapacity is in question. After a maximum of six months of continuous incapacity to work or if incapacity to work lasted twelve discontinued months over the past eighteen months, the Republic Fund for Health Insurance is mandated to send the employee in question to the competent body for an official assessment of his/her capabilities to work, that is, state of disability, in accordance with the regulations governing pension and disability insurance. In this case, the Fund bears the costs of salary compensation until the day of the determination of invalidity but not longer than sixty days from the day of submission of the request for the initiation of this procedure. Following this period, the compensation costs have to be covered by the Pension Fund, which is obliged to inform the Fund of its findings.[176]

---

174. *See* Art. 76, paras 4 and 5 of the Act on Health Insurance.
175. As stipulated in the Act on Labour, Art. 103, para. 5, as well as in Arts 150, 152 and 154 of the Act on Health Insurance.
176. *See* Arts 80 and 81 of the Act on Health Insurance.

Chapter 4. Amounts of Benefits

§1. Wage Earners

204. The method for settling accounts and paying compensation for sick leave is regulated both by the Act on Labour and by the Act on Health Insurance. The reason for this is that compensation for the first thirty days is paid and financed by the employer, and after that by the Republic Fund for Health Insurance. There are exceptions to these guidelines – the employer provides compensation during the entire period in the case of occupational injury and occupational disease. Contrary to this, compensation from the first day of incapacity to work is provided for by the Fund for voluntary organ donors and for persons caring for sick children under the age of 3. In reality, the employer always pays compensation after receiving the payment from the Fund. The Fund is obliged to make compensation payments available to the employer within thirty days at the latest, from the day of the receipt of the invoice. The Republic Fund for Health Insurance pays compensation exclusively for private employees, to women in connection with pregnancy and maternity (caring for sick children).[177]

205. The amount of compensation for the first thirty days of sickness benefit is determined by the Act on Labour. In accordance with Article 115 of the Act on Labour, the benefit amount equals:

- 65% of the income that the employee would have made in last three months when they were temporarily incapacitated, if the incapacity to work was caused by illness or injury outside of the workplace (the amount of compensation cannot be lower than minimum income in accordance with the Act on Labour);
- 100% of the same income, if the incapacity was caused by an accident at work or an occupational disease (the minimum is the same as above).[178]

206. The Fund for Health Insurance makes compensation payments, in the same amounts as above, of the income that the employee (insured person) would have made in the last twelve months when the person was temporarily incapacitated (the income comprises the basic wage of the employee, part of earnings for working performance and the increased wage for each year spent at work with the employer in accordance with the Act on Labour).[179] The entitlement amount is also 100% for voluntary tissue and organ donors. The basis for determining the amount of the compensation payment, if the insured person has not made any income for twelve

177. *See* Arts 101 and 102 of the Act on Health Insurance.
178. In case the insured person is suspended from work during the time period in which they enjoy the right to receive compensation payments, due to being charged with a criminal offence or held in custody as well as in some other cases regulated by law, compensation payment is paid in the amount which equals one fourth of previously set compensation payment and if the insured person supports the members of his/her close family the compensation payment equals one third of the set payment.
179. Article 108 of the Act on Labour sets forth 0.4% wage increase for each year of employment with the employer.

months, is the average amount of previously received payments. If the employer temporarily fails to pay the workers, they are still entitled to compensation in the amount of the minimum income, in accordance with the same law. If the employer pays their salaries upon completion of the work in question, then the compensation amount will be determined in the usual way. Insured persons on part-time employment contracts are entitled to compensation proportional to their hours worked.[180]

207. All beneficiaries are entitled to salary compensation starting from the first day and continuing as long as the period of incapacity to work lasts, but only during the time period in which the insured person would normally receive a salary. In other words, termination of the person's employment contract creates a termination of the compensation payments. The right to salary compensation also ends in the case when the final decision on long-term invalidity becomes effective. As an exception, if the temporary incapacity to work is caused by an injury at work or an occupational disease, the insured person is entitled to salary compensation from the first day and throughout the duration of the incapacity.[181]

208. There are also limits regarding the entitlement to salary compensation in cases concerning caring for a sick family member. Compensation is paid in the following cases:

- when caring for a sick member of the immediate family under the age of 7 or older member with disability – not longer than fifteen days;
- if the sick person is over the age of 7 – not longer than seven days;
- when there are justifiable health reasons, the compensation period related to caring for a member of the immediate family can be even longer: if the sick person is under the age of 7 or person with disability, compensation is paid for up to thirty days; if the sick person is over the age of 7, entitlement to compensation payments lasts for up to fourteen days; in case of serious diseases of the child under the age of 18, entitlement to compensation payments can be extended to four months (and can be renewed, as assessed by the Commission.[182]

209. The only condition for compensation for care of family members is that both parents work, or that the child has only one parent. There is also a provision for the situation where one parent does not work but health reasons prevent him/her from caring for the child, thereby forcing the working parent to stay at home and care for the sick child. Such an insured person qualifies for compensation. This right also refers to adoptive parents, foster parents, step-fathers and step-mothers.[183]

180. *See* Arts 86–87 and Arts 95–97 of the Act on Health Insurance.
181. *See* Art. 101 of the Act on Health Insurance.
182. *See* Art. 78 of the Act on Health Insurance.
183. *See* Art. 79 of the Act on Health Insurance.

§2. Self-Employed Workers

210. Benefits for incapacity to work for self-employed persons, farmers and agricultural workers differ from the ones that apply for wage earners, since the method of contribution calculations differ as well. The basis for compensation for this group consists of an average monthly basis for which health insurance contributions are paid, as determined by the twelve-month period preceding the period in which the sickness or injury occurred. If the period of employment is shorter, the basis is calculated taking into account the time spent as being insured. If the self-employed person did not engage in any business activities in the twelve-month period, the calculation basis for compensation is determined by applying the lowest prescribed basis.[184]

211. If the period of incapacity to work lasts for more than two months, the basis for compensation for every succeeding month is adjusted for the fluctuations in the average monthly salary per employee within the territory of the Republic. The amount of compensation is the same as for wage earners, 65% or 100% of the basis, depending on the cause of the incapacity to work (*see* above). Compensation to the self-employed and their workers is paid exclusively by the Republic Fund for Health Insurance.[185]

184. *See* Art. 89 of the Act on Health Insurance.
185. *See* Arts 95 and 102 of the Act on Health Insurance.

Chapter 5. Conditions

212. The conditions for entitlement to cash benefits under health insurance are the same as for healthcare (*see* above). They include insurance registration, insurance period (three months in continuity or six months in discontinuity), an issued and certified health card and contributions paid. In addition, in order to receive some of the financial benefits, appropriate documentation must be submitted (a formal request is necessary).[186]

213. To receive sick leave compensation, one needs:

– a report from the competent doctor or medical committee certifying the inability or incapacity to work;
– confirmation from the employer of the worker's salary to serve as the calculation basis for determining the compensation amount;
– confirmation from the employer of the worker's total hours in the last month, in the case that the incapacitated worker works part-time.[187]

214. To receive compensation for transportation, the following documents have to be submitted:

– confirmation of the need for such transportation certified by the health institution;
– proof of the cost of transportation, as requested.[188]

215. For compensation for incapacity to work, the law makes provisions for grounds for exclusion. These are:

– if incapacity to work has been caused intentionally;
– if incapacity to work is caused by acute alcoholism or use of psychotropic substances;
– if the beneficiary intentionally tried to prevent recovery, that is regaining the capability to work;
– if the beneficiary refuses to undergo medical treatment without a satisfactory reason;
– if the beneficiary fails to report to a doctor for an assessment of their working capabilities, or fails to attend scheduled doctor's appointments or medical committee examinations;
– if the beneficiary engages in any income generating activities during the period that they are officially incapacitated to work;

186. *See* Art. 109 of the Act on Health Insurance and Arts 80–87 of the Regulation on Conditions and Means of Acquiring Health Insurance Entitlements.
187. *See* more details in Art. 81 of the Regulation on Conditions and Means of Acquiring Health Insurance Entitlements.
188. *See* Art. 87 of the Regulation on Conditions and Means of Acquiring Health Insurance Entitlements.

– if the beneficiary leaves his/her place of residence without permission of the medical committee of the branch office of the Fund;
– if he/she receives compensation on the ground of some other regulation;
– if in any other way he/she abuses the right to absence from work due to incapacity to work.

216. Also, salary compensations are not due to persons serving prison time and those against whom such security measures as mandatory psychiatric treatment and confinement in psychiatric wards have been taken, as well as alcoholics and drug addicts receiving mandatory treatment in health institutions. Their entitlement to salary compensation terminates on the day of the establishment of the aforementioned conditions and lasts until they have been resolved.[189]

217. If the beneficiary falls ill with the same illness within a six-day period following the end of his/her period of incapacity to work, or if the person becomes sick from another illness the next day upon ending the period of incapacity to work, it is considered an extension of the original incapacity (and, therefore, counted as such in terms of the calculation basis for compensation, the amount of compensation and the entity paying).[190]

189. *See* Art. 84 of the Act on Health Insurance.
190. *See* Art. 75 of the Act on Health Insurance.

Chapter 6. Accumulation Rules

218. The general rule in the social security system in Serbia is that a person cannot benefit from different entitlements based on the same risk, except when those entitlements are compatible; that is, when they can be used simultaneously in practice (e.g., medical treatment, compensation due to incapacity to work and professional rehabilitation in case of injury at work). In addition, there can be no accumulation of wages, maternity and incapacity to work benefits. Private insurance compensation can be combined with statutory benefits, as well as benefits from voluntary health insurances with the State health insurance.

219. It is also assumed that the beneficiary cannot exercise the same right at two different office branches of the health insurance institution (e.g., one at the office branch in the work location, and the other at the office branch at the place of residence). The prevention of such incidents is under the competence of the institution's ex officio. In the case that it may still occur, the insured person is obliged to return the resources, and may also be prosecuted for criminal offences.

Part VI. Industrial Accidents and Occupational Diseases

220. Insurance against industrial accidents and occupational diseases in Serbia has traditionally been regulated together with the system of old-age and survivor's pensions. This is the reason why both of these segments of social security are administered by the same institution – the Pension and Disability Insurance Fund (*see* further).

221. A distinguishing feature is that the above-named branch in Serbia covers employees not only in the case of incapacity to work due to industrial accidents and occupational diseases, but also due to injury and illness outside of the work place. In reality the requirements to qualify for these rights are stricter for the latter types of risks and provide less benefits.

222. This branch of social security is one of the oldest and most important in Serbia. Around 2000, it was the cause of a huge financial burden for the State Health Insurance considering that the number of disability pensioners reached 32.2% of the total number of pensioners in Serbia. This percentage is lower at present, since conditions for acquiring a disability pension became very strict in 2003, so that it is very difficult to get the disability pension today.[191] Such circumstances are partially a consequence of the declining quality of protections at work due to the general crisis. Additionally, it is to a great extent caused by the fact that the problem of the labour surplus in the 1990s was resolved by sending employees into invalidity retirement. An exceedingly light set of conditions to qualify for being incapacitated to work on the part of the social security administration also worked in favour of this kind of solution. This is why the requirements for the eligibility for benefits from this branch have been made much stricter in the Act on Pension and Disability Insurance of Serbia of 2 April 2003, and the control of the determination of incapacity to work has also become stricter. However, despite such strict control, there were numerous instances of abuse. Understanding the extent of the abuse, near the

---

191. On an average, one out of four disability pension's requirements is approved. The number of disability pensioners in November 2018 was 287,287. *See*: *Invalidity Pensions: The List Is Shorter for 150,000 Names (Invalidske penzije: Lista kraća za 150.000 imena)*, *Večernje novosti online* (daily newspaper), 14 Nov. 2018, http://www.novosti.rs/vesti/naslovna/drustvo/aktuelno.290.html:760518-Invalidske-penzije-Lista-kraca-za-150000-imena; *Rigorous Conditions for Pension (Rigorozni uslovi za penziju)*, *Naslovi net*, 22 Nov. 2009, www.naslovi.net/2009-11-22/mondo/rigorozni-uslovi-za-invalidsku-penziju/1419650.

end of 2014, the Government has initiated a revision of pensions (examining thoroughly whether all relevant conditions in acquiring disability pensions were met as well as the lawfulness of the pertinent procedure. As a result, by October 2015, 244 disability pensions were drawn back. At the same time, 2,091 disability pensions were validated.[192]

192. *See*: Anticipated revision of Disability pensions in the forthcoming period (*Uskoro revizija invalidskih penzija,* RTV (television – online), 5 Sep. 2014, http://www.rtv.rs/sr_lat/ekonomija/uskoro-revizija-invalidskih-penzija_516353.html; Revision of Disability Pensions– *Huge Work Yet to Be Done* (*Revizija invalidskih penzija – veliki posao tek predstoji),* RTS (television – online), 4 Oct. 2015, http://www.rts.rs/page/stories/sr/story/125/Društvo/2051094/Revizija+invalidskih+penzija,+veliki+posao+tek+predstoji.html.

Chapter 1. Field of Application

§1. Territorial Field of Application

223. The system of insurance against industrial accidents and occupational diseases applies primarily within the territory of the country. As an exception, this insurance also covers domestic workers working abroad for domestic (détaché – posted workers) or foreign employers, in the case that they are not insured there or their benefits do not extend beyond the territory of the country (*see* above).

§2. Personal Field of Application

224. Specifically for Serbia, the group of individuals covered by disability insurance is somewhat wider than that which would be expected, extending beyond wage earners and self-employed persons (including independent agricultural workers – farmers) to cover others as well.[193] These are:

- persons in temporary or occasional employment;
- redundant workers receiving unemployment benefits;
- persons performing jobs for the public benefit (rescue workers, military drills and other exercises in the area of defence of the country, youth work drives, work camps or competition, other jobs for the general interest such as 'public works' or performing public functions);
- volunteers;
- persons on job-specialization training and vocational re-training;
- apprentices and trainees;
- persons working while serving prison sentences;
- persons on contracts for additional work, contract by work or other contracts on the basis of which they receive financial compensation.[194]

225. There is a certain difference among these categories regarding the risks covered, in the sense that some of them are not insured against profession-related diseases. However, since the persons in question are not realistically in a position to be exposed to profession-related diseases due to the short duration of their work, in practice this difference is of no significance.

---

193. The term 'independent agricultural workers' has been used in Serbian legislation for a long time and it actually refers to farmers and other persons employed in agriculture. These terms are not even now completely set apart (insurance refers to both groups) so henceforth these terms will be mentioned alternatively.
194. *See* Arts 11–14 and 254 of the Act on Pension and Disability Insurance.

Chapter 2. Concept of 'Industrial Accident'

226. In accordance with Article 22 of the Act on Pension and Disability Insurance, injury at work is considered to be such injury to the insured that occurs in a spatial, temporal and causal connection with the performance of the job that is the basis for insurance, caused by direct and quick mechanical, physical or chemical action, rapid changes of body position, sudden burdening to the body or other physiological changes to the body.

227. Two key elements of the concept of injury at work from the legal definition are:

(1) accident; and
(2) linked with the contract of employment.

§1. Accident

228. In order to avoid confusion in practice, the mentioned law contains an exact list of possible ways of becoming injured at work. These are injuries caused by:

- direct and quick mechanical, physical or chemical action;
- rapid changes of body position;
- sudden burdening to the body or other physiological changes of the state of the body.

229. Additionally, the concept of injury at work has also been extended to cover the insured person's illness caused by an accident or force majeure during the performance of work on the basis of which the person was insured, or related to this work.

230. Thus, the basic condition for determining the existence of an injury at work is that it was impossible to predict or prevent, as well as that it occurred suddenly; that is, the damaging event lasted a short amount of time. An accident does not necessarily cause incapacity to work or death. It is qualified as such even if it only causes an injury requiring medical attention.

§2. Link to the Contract of Employment

231. An accident becomes an industrial accident if it shows spatial, temporal and causal connection with the job that is the basis for insurance. This primarily means that it has to occur at the workplace and in connection with the contracted job. However, since practice has shown that accidents are possible in some other situations related to the contract of employment, the following are also considered to be industrial accidents:

- accidents that occurred on another job which the employee performed in the interest of the employer;
- that occurred on business trips or on the way to work;
- that occurred in connection with exercising the right to health protection caused by occupational injury or by occupational sickness;
- that occurred in connection with the right to placement or employment at a different appropriate job, or to vocational re-training;
- that occurred while conducting previously mentioned activities within the public interest;
- that occurred during natural disasters or catastrophes.[195]

232. The victim does not have to prove that the accident, which happened at work or in connection with work, was caused by the execution of a contract of employment. This is ex officio conducted by the insurance administration in a procedure initiated at the insured person's request. If the person is not satisfied with his/her evaluation of the event, the victim may appeal to an appellate body within the insurance fund, and after that to the court system.

233. Whether the accident was the worker's own fault has no bearing on pronouncing the existence of an industrial accident, even if it was caused by extremely negligent behaviour.

§3. Accidents on the Way to Work

234. Injuries sustained by the insured on their regular route from home to work and back are also considered industrial accidents. There is no precise definition of a 'regular' way to work – it has been left to the competent body of the court to decide on this matter in cases of dispute. It is not necessarily the shortest route, but courts also do not take 'regular way to work' to mean atypical, that is, unusual departures from that route.

195. *See* Arts 22 and 23 of the Act on Pension and Disability Insurance.

Chapter 3. Concept of 'Occupational Disease'

235. The concept of occupational disease is determined in two ways: First, a general, legal definition of disease has to be determined. Second, an official list of diseases has to be created. In order to qualify as occupational disease, each individual case has to fit within these two frames.

236. In accordance with Article 24 of the Act on Pension and Disability Insurance, professional diseases are those that:

- developed during the insurance period;
- were caused by the extended immediate effects from the processes and conditions of work on jobs performed by the insured person.

237. The most important element of this definition, the one that has to be proved by the victim, is that he/she was exposed to the negative effects for an extended period of time. Another important condition is that the disease conforms to the requirements set by the Regulation on Determining Professional Diseases, of 6 March 2019.[196] This Regulation determines the following:

- the list of profession-related diseases (including diseases caused by exposure to chemicals, physical matters, biological factors, lung diseases, skin and malignant diseases);[197]
- posts and jobs where these diseases might manifest themselves;
- medical conditions under which certain diseases qualify as 'occupational'.[198]

238. Only if the disease meets all of the requirements laid out in the Regulation may the employee receive benefits from the 'occupational risk insurance'. Unfortunately, Serbian legislation has not yet accepted the so-called mixed system of occupational diseases that has been introduced into many European countries. This means that there is no option for the victim to prove the origin of his/her disease if it is not on the official list.

196. Published in the Official Herald of the RS, No. 14/2019.
197. There are sixty-four occupational diseases on this list.
198. Article 1 of the Regulation. This list was based on the ILO (International Labour Organization) Employment Injury Convention, No. 121, of 1964, which was ratified by Yugoslavia on 7 May 1970. (Published in the Official Gazette of the SFRY, International Agreements, No. 27/1970.)

Chapter 4. Medical Care

239. A victim of an industrial accident or occupational disease is entitled to free medical care for as long as it is required. The care can be combined with special medical rehabilitation with the aim of enabling the victim to participate in further professional activities and with special professional rehabilitation of invalids (*see* further).[199]There is a special law regarding this matter in Serbia – Act on Professional Rehabilitation and Employment of Disabled Persons and the Act on Social Protection of 4 April 2011.[200] Health protection of these individuals applies under the same conditions as for other health insurance beneficiaries, with the reservation that persons who suffer injury at work or a professional disease are entitled to preferential treatment. They are released from participating in the costs of treatment. In addition, during their temporary incapacity to work, they receive maximum compensation (100% of their former salary). It is the employer's obligation to provide this compensation throughout the entire period of incapacity (*see* above). The costs of treatment and medical rehabilitation are completely covered by the institution for health insurance.

---

199. *See* Regulation on Conditions, Criteria and Standards for Professional Rehabilitation, (Arts 4 and 11), Published in the Official Herald of the RS, No. 112/2009.
200. The Act is published in: Official Herald of the RS, Nos 36/2009, 32/2013.

Chapter 5. Incapacity to Work

240. Industrial accidents and professional diseases can be the cause of partial or total incapacity to work that is of a temporary or permanent nature. In the case of temporary incapacity, treatment and benefits during the period of incapacity are provided within the health insurance system. Regarding permanent incapacity, entitlements relating to taking care of the victim are under the jurisdiction of the pension and disability insurance institutions. The assessment and determination of incapacity are conducted by specialized committees of doctors (expert's reporting bodies) for each social security branch separately.

§1. Temporary Total Incapacity

241. In the period immediately following the accident, the victim is usually completely unable to work. As in other cases concerning incapacity to work due to weakened health, the entire period of incapacity is covered by the employer in accordance with the Act on the Health Insurance (*see* above). If his/her employment is terminated or if the person is self-employed, compensation is financed by health insurance institutions (*see* above).[201] The benefit amount is the highest possible – 100% of the victim's salary prior to becoming incapacitated – and is paid until health is restored; that is, until the victim is able to return to work (compensation is paid even in cases of termination of the employment).[202]

242. If, however, there are grounds to suspect that the case may not be temporary, but rather permanent incapacity to work, the victim will be referred for a re-assessment of his/her working capabilities either immediately or after a few months (but not later than six months of continual incapacity to work or twelve discontinued months over the period of past eighteen months) of sick leave. The evaluation is conducted by bodies of reporting experts from the branch of invalidity insurance (*see* above).[203]

§2. Temporary Partial Incapacity

243. The regulations on health insurance in Serbia stipulate that, if the physician deems that work would be beneficial and would help re-establish full working capabilities, the victim may work part-time for a period of time (four hours daily at least). This kind of work may last at the most for three consecutive months or a year with interruptions (*see* above).[204]

201. *See* Art. 101 of the Act on Health Insurance.
202. *See* Art. 101, para. 3 of the Act on Health Insurance.
203. *See* Art. 80 of the Act on Health Insurance.
204. *See* Art. 98 of the Act on Health Insurance.

§3. PERMANENT INCAPACITY

244. In more severe cases, the accident can cause a permanent loss of capacity to work, either partial or total. In those situations, financial compensation to the victims of the accident at work or the profession-related disease falls under the jurisdiction of the pension and disability insurance institutions. Treatment remains under the jurisdiction of the health insurance branch.

245. Permanent incapacity to work is termed 'invalidity' in Serbian legislation. In accordance with Article 21 of the Act on Pension and Disability Insurance, 'invalidity' is the condition when the insured person's capacity to perform his/her job becomes permanently lost due to changes in health caused by an accident at work, professional disease, injury outside the workplace or diseases that cannot be cured through treatment or medical rehabilitation.

246. The loss of capacity to work is the case when the wage earner or self-employed (also farmers/the independent agricultural workers) insured person becomes completely and permanently incapacitated and cannot perform the job.

247. Based on former regulations, invalidity implied both the loss of capacity to work and 'the reduction of capacity to work' (when the employee still partially retains the capabilities of performing the job, so-called residual working capacity). 'Residual working capacity' was the condition in which wage earners or self-employed workers (excluding independent agricultural workers/farmers) were capable of performing other appropriate types of work, without overtly straining themselves, at least half-time or for which they could be re-trained to perform.[205] In addition to the obligatory reassignment to other jobs, these persons had 'the right to salary differential compensation' (if disabled persons received lower salaries at their new jobs). According to the new Act brought in 2003, these rights are maintained in Serbia and applied to employed persons categorized as work invalids with a residual capacity to work until the elimination of this category. If, the unemployed persons or person who in the meantime lost status of insured person entitled to these rights they receive disability pensions instead of these rights (amounting half of disability pension).[206]

248. A person who loses the capacity to work can become entitled to:

– a disability pension;
– an allowance for assistance and care.[207]

205. In accordance with Art. 38, para. 3 of the former federal Act that governed this area – Act on the Bases of Pension and Disability Insurance, of 28 Jun. 1996 (Official Gazette of the FRY, Nos 30/96, 58/98, 70/2001, 3/2002, 39/2002, 5/2003), another appropriate job is considered to be a job which, according to his/her qualifications and residual working capacity, the insured person is capable of performing full-time with an overall effort that would not endanger his/her health.

206. *See* Arts 222–226 of the Act on Pension and Disability Insurance.

207. *See* Arts 41a and 75a of the Act on Pension and Disability Insurance.

249. The right to a disability pension is determined in the same way as old-age pension (*see* further) with the provision that the victim of an occupational accident or profession-related disease will be entitled to a disability pension under more relaxed rules than other insured persons. That person will be entitled to a pension regardless of the length of his/her contribution payments. Also, the disability pension is the amount that a person with a forty-year contribution period would receive.[208]

250. Persons whose incapacity to work was caused by injuries or diseases stemming from incidents outside of the workplace need to have an appropriate length of service in order to qualify for a disability pension. If the condition of invalidity began after the age of 30, the insurance period has to be five years. If invalidity occurred prior to that, the requirements are as follows:

- before the age of 20 – an insurance period of at least a year;
- before the age of 25 – two years of insurance;
- before the age of 30 – at least three years of insurance.[209]

251. Work invalids whose incapacity to work was caused by injuries incurred outside of the workplace have a slightly more favourable pension in Serbia than other insured persons. In the process of their pension calculation, a certain number of years, depending on the individual's age, are added to their contribution period (despite the fact that contributions have not been paid for the particular year).[210]

252. Disability pensions are administered by the pension and disability insurance institutions – Republic Fund for Pension and Disability Insurance (and Provincial Fund for Pension and Disability Insurance – in the Province of Vojvodina). Expenses are covered by the insurance institution.[211]

253. In addition to disability, there is another social risk that is covered by this branch of social security and which can be the result of an injury or disease – 'bodily harm'. In accordance with Article 37 of the Act on Pension and Disability Insurance, bodily harm is diagnosed when the loss, major impairment or significant incapacitation of certain organs or body parts occurs, having a debilitating effect on normal bodily activities and requiring more effort in conducting regular daily activities, whether or not it causes invalidity. In other words, this risk is not dependent on the insured person's ability to work.

254. Bodily harm can be classified within the range of 30%–100%. In order to fall under this category, any health deterioration has to be mentioned in the list established by Regulation on Determining Physical Handicap, of 28 October

208. *See* Arts 61 and 69 of the Act on Pension and Disability Insurance.
209. *See* Arts 25 and 26 of the Act on Pension and Disability Insurance.
210. *See* Art. 69 of the Act on Pension and Disability Insurance.
211. Entitlements are provided by the branch office where the insured person was insured at the time of injury.

2003.[212] If it is caused by an accident at work or a profession-related disease and the capacity is classified to be at least 30%, the insured persons are entitled to additional financial compensation. The compensation amount is directly proportionate to the percentage of bodily harm. These payments are made from the basis, which makes up 25% of the average monthly net salary per employee in the Republic in the preceding year. Compensation for bodily harm continues to be paid even after retirement, provided that it was incurred during work.

255. In order to avoid the negative effects of inflation, all compensations and financial amounts received by the victim are regularly adjusted. In accordance with Articles 80 and 81 of the Act on Pension and Disability Insurance, disability pensions and the financial compensation for bodily harm (and other pensions) are adjusted every 1 April and 1 October, according to the cost of living in the six preceding months.[213] Since 2014 these regulations have practically been suspended. An amendment to the Law has been made and according to Article 80b pensions are to be harmonized in the way which is regulated by the acts applied to administer the budget and budget system until financial sustainability of the pension and disability pension system is achieved. The Law on changes and amendments to the Law on the Budget system from 25 December 2014 establishes that pension rise is possible only during the year in which it is expected and estimated that the pension budget will equal up to 11% of gross domestic product (GDP) taking into account that this budget does not exceed this percentage in GDP after harmonizing.

212. Official Herald of the RS, Nos 105/2003, 120/2008.

213. Exceptionally, if the gross national product in the previous calendar year rises more than 4%, then the pensions are adjusted from 1 April of the current year according to the percentage obtained from consumer price index rates and gross product.

Chapter 6. Death

256. In the case that the victim of the industrial accident or occupational disease dies, the survivors (dependants) can claim certain rights. They are entitled to a survivor's pension (*see* further). If the death occurs as a consequence of 'occupational risks', the survivors are entitled to a pension under more favourable conditions than other insured persons – regardless of the contribution period previously acquired by the victim.[214]

257. If the disability or other type of pension beneficiary dies, the person who covers burial costs is provided with compensation for these costs in the amount of 150% of the average pension as calculated for the last three months.[215]

214. Other cases are conditioned on at least a five-year active insurance period. *See* Art. 25 of the Act on Pension and Disability Insurance.
215. *See* Arts 41 and 75 of the Act on Pension and Disability Insurance.

Chapter 7. Prevention of Occupational Diseases

258. Former Serbian legislation law provided a few preventive measures to avoid occupational disease or invalidity. There were two special risks in connection with preventive measures:

– changed capacity to work;
– direct danger of becoming disabled.

If there were signs that these risks were imminent, the insured person could automatically become entitled to relocation to another job for which he/she has the capacity and qualifications to perform.

259. Changed capacity to work was the condition where an insured person was not considered a work invalid, but permanent changes in his/her health condition prevented the person from safely conducting the jobs. Direct danger of becoming disabled existed when the working conditions, despite existing preventive measures at work, affected the health and working capabilities of the employee to such a degree that there was a reason to believe that he/she would become disabled if continuing to perform that particular job. In that case, employees were entitled to a job change with vocational re-training if needed. They were also entitled to salary differential compensation due to a lower salary at the new job.

260. As of 28 December 2001 (when amendments were made to the last Federal Act on Pension and Disability Insurance) the risk 'direct danger of becoming disabled' was eliminated in Serbia. However, there are some provisions for partial preventive measures in the labour law. The Act on Labour of 2005 (Article 101) stipulates that employees with health problems developed during work, in the case of disability or direct danger of becoming disabled, must be transferred to other jobs.

Chapter 8. Supplementary Benefits

261. In Serbia, pension and disability insurance is still run almost exclusively by the State. This is why there are no problems related to the adjustment of benefits to reflect changes in the costs of living, which sometimes arise in systems where only private disability insurance exists. Consequently, there is no need for 'supplementary benefits' that serve as protection of work invalids standards in the countries that have private disability insurance (it should be pointed out that in general all pensions in Serbia are relatively low). However, some rights and guarantees resembling supplementary benefits have been established with the same protective aim. First, regular adjustments against consumer prices (formerly known as the costs of living) have been stipulated in the Act on Pension and Disability Insurance[216] for all financial benefits. Also, a protective minimum has been established. The pension adjusted in this way cannot be lower than 27% of the average salary within the territory of the Republic in the preceding year.[217]

262. The victim of the occupational accident or disease is also protected when his/her health condition deteriorates. In that case, a re-evaluation of the capacity to work takes place.

216. Amendments of the Act on Pension and Disability Insurance of 29 Dec. 2010 anticipated exceptional rise of pensions in 2011, allowing 1% rise of pensions in total. Also, the lowest pension for retired farmers was set at RSD 9,000 (about EUR 90), implying that subsequent changes and adjustments to consumer prices will be made regularly. *See* Art. 76 of the Act on Pension and Disability Insurance.

217. *See* Art. 76 of the Act on Pension and Disability Insurance.

Chapter 9. No-Fault Insurance

263. Regarding the right to benefits from occupational risks insurance, the basic principle is that the fault of the employer or of the victim plays no role whatsoever. The employee does not have to prove the fault of any person to qualify for benefits.

264. This, however, does not mean that the employer or the persons who caused the accident are completely free of liabilities toward the insurance institution. In Serbia, the regulations force the person at fault to refund the Pension and Disability Insurance Fund for all of the costs related to the injury or occupational disease (treatment, rehabilitation or other compensation). The employer is liable if the reason for the injury at work or occupational disease occurred due to the employer's failure to take appropriate measures for the protection of health and safety at work.[218] The Pension and Disability Insurance Fund can request compensation for damages from the insurance company as well, if the damage occurred through usage of a motor vehicle.

---

218. The Pension and Disability Insurance Fund has to demand the compensation from employer. When determining the cost of damages, amounts of paid contributions are not taken into consideration. *See* Art. 208 of the Act on Pension and Disability Insurance.

Chapter 10. Civil Liability

265. The fact that the victim can enjoy rights from the insurance against professional risks does not exclude rights to civil liability claims. The employer, a fellow worker or any other person who caused the injury or disease can be considered liable. Insurance companies can also be held liable. When determining the amount of damages to be paid, the court has to take into consideration the victim's income from regular and disability insurance.[219]

266. Civil liability due to death, injury or disease is covered by the legislation on contracts and torts, and is regulated by the former federal Act on Contracts and Torts of 25 May 1978 (*see* above). In accordance with the provisions of this law, damage compensations can be not only to the victim, but also to the family members and persons the victim supported or aided on a regular basis – spouse or partner, children, parents, siblings. Compensation may cover the costs of treatment, loss of current and future salaries due to incapacity or reduced capacity to work, reduced possibilities to develop and advance professionally, as well as compensation for having endured physical and mental anguish, overall decrease of life activities and possible burial costs.[220]

267. As a rule, damages are awarded in the form of monthly payments, either for life or for limited duration. If there are justified grounds (e.g., if there is reason to doubt that the debtor is going to pay the rent in the future) the rent can be paid in a single instalment. If circumstances change in the meantime, the compensation amount in the form of can be either reduced or cancelled.

219. There are numerous examples of judicial practice in the field of damage compensation caused by such events.
220. Articles 193, 195, 200, 201 of the Act on Contracts and Torts.

Chapter 11. Accumulation Rules

268. The legislation on industrial accidents and occupational diseases does not contain precise non-accumulation rules concerning the combination of benefits under the social insurance and civil liability compensation. However, from the Act on Contracts and Torts, it follows that nobody can collect a greater amount from a single event than the damages caused by the said event. There is an exception to this rule if the person has concluded Life Insurance Contract with the insurance company and is therefore receiving increased compensation (these contracts have become an increasingly common practice over the past few years). In other words, civil liability compensation can be combined with benefits under social insurance only if they do not cover the same or complete damages.

269. In most cases in practice, compensation from industrial accident insurance will be paid first. Civil liability damage is usually realized later in lengthy proceedings before the court. As a rule, the courts accept the assessment of a worker's capacity to work by the social insurance institutions, except in the case that the victim disagrees with the assessment.

270. As far as exercising rights from 'occupational insurance' while receiving a salary or enjoying other social benefits, the rules are clear. Most often these earnings exclude one another, but there are some situations when certain benefits can accompany disability pension (e.g., compensation for bodily harm, care allowance).

271. Considering that work invalids are categorized as invalids with a complete loss of the capacity to work, the legislation stipulates that such persons do not have the right to engage professionally in other jobs. If they do, the body that provided the expert's report on the individual's capacity to work is required to schedule another appointment. If the re-assessment concludes that the person in question is able to work again, their pension entitlement is revoked.

Part VII. Unemployment

272. This branch of social security in Serbia, as in most countries, contains two different sets of rules. The first concerns actions to provide the unemployed person with a job (active measures). The other part is standard unemployment insurance that provides unemployment benefit aiming to help the unemployed person bridge the period when he/she has no means of income (so-called passive measures). Reforms in this area, initiated fourteen years ago, were focused on more proactive employment policy. This new policy necessitated a much more active role on behalf of all participants in the employment process (the State, State employment administration and unemployed person). It also introduced more rigid criteria in granting benefits and made it clear that the unemployed persons are expected to take more active role in their search for job and accept jobs offered to them or else lose the benefits. This Reform was initiated by the Act on Employment and Insurance against Unemployment of 15 July 2003,[221] and continued with the Act on Employment and Insurance against Unemployment of 15 May 2009.[222] Both documents were inspired by the practice in member countries of the European Union. However, it should be noted that the present unemployment rate in Serbia is quite high (in reality close to 20%),[223] and on the constant rise over the past few years.

273. In practice, unemployment rights are administered, under the supervision of the competent ministries, by unemployment institution – National Employment Administration, through branch offices. In 2010, the Administration Headquarters were moved from the capital Belgrade to the town of Kragujevac thus initiating the decentralization process of State institutions.[224]

In the Province of Vojvodina, as a constituent part all activities related to employment within its territory are managed by the Provincial Employment Administration (in the name of the National Employment Administration).

221. *See* above.
222. Published in the Official Herald of the RS, Nos 36/2009, 88/2010, 38/2015, 113/2017, 113/2017.
223. Formal unemployment in 2019 is 12.1%, but the problem is that the employment rate is low – 47.4%, which shows that the unemployment issue is much bigger than presented by the government (*see National Bureau of Statistics, Anketa o radnoj snazi (Labour Force Survey)*, http://www.stat.gov.rs/sr-Latn/oblasti/trziste-rada/anketa-o-radnoj-snazi. Experts in this field assume that percentage of unemployment is higher than statistically calculated. *See Nezaposlenost nepovoljnija od one koju prikazuje statistika (Unemployment Is Less Favorable than That Shown by Statistics)*, N1 (Television news portal), 3 Aug. 2017, http://rs.n1info.com/Biznis/a288290/Nezaposlenost-nepovoljnija-od-one-koju-prikazuje-statistika.html.
224. *See* Amendments of the Act on Employment and Insurance against Unemployment of 23 Nov. 2010 (published in the Official Herald of the RS, No. 88/2010).

Chapter 1. Provision of Work

§1. Labour Mediation

274. In accordance with the Act on Employment and Insurance against Unemployment, labour mediation in Serbia is understood as a part of active employment policy to mean providing expert assistance in finding employment within the country and abroad by a branch office of the National Employment Administration and by private employment agencies that have met all of the legal conditions required to perform such services.[225] The right to labour mediation refers primarily to the unemployed, but it can also cover employed persons under certain circumstances (e.g., if they do not have a stable job or a job that corresponds with their education and training).[226] In order to improve labour mediation, in accordance with the Act on Employment, employers are obliged to report every free post to the National Employment Administration (at the same time, they do have the right to employ a person without mediation by the Administration or any other agency).[227] Also, mediation services have to be free of charge for the unemployed (or possibly covered by the employer), whereas employed persons who are looking for another job through an agency can be charged a mediation fee if the process of finding this new job inflicted unexpected expenses (e.g., for training or education).

275. The method of labour mediation is described in greater detail in the internal regulations of the National Employment Administration, among which the Regulation on the Criteria, the Way and Other Relevant Issues of Proactive Measures of Employment Policy, of 11 December 2015 is the most important.[228] Labour mediation is made by connecting directly employers and employees seeking jobs and by providing expert help to employees seeking to change jobs. In accordance with Article 6 of the aforementioned Regulation, direct association of employers and employees seeking jobs is done in one of the following ways:

- by an interview with the person seeking employment;
- by assessment of the employability and by helping the unemployed person to make his/her own employment plan;
- by connecting people seeking employment with the employers on the labour market;
- by making preliminary selection of employees on behalf of the employer;
- by providing a training in techniques of active searching for jobs;
- by group representation of information on employment opportunities;

225. Besides labour mediation, the Act (Art. 43) anticipates the following proactive employment policy measures: (1) help in choosing the right profession (professional orientation) and subsequent career counselling; (2) subsidies for new posts offered to unemployed persons; (3) support to self-employed persons; (4) additional education and training; (5) incentive measures for beneficiaries of financial aid; (6) public works; (7) other measures taken to facilitate employment of unemployed persons seeking jobs.
226. *See* Art. 44 para. 3 and Art. 3 of the Act on Employment and Insurance against Unemployment.
227. *See* Arts 35 and 93 of the Act on Employment and Insurance against Unemployment.
228. Published in the Official Herald of the RS, Nos. 71/2015, 5/2017, 9/2018.

- by organizing 'employment exhibitions';
- by implementation of inter-regional labour mediation; and
- in a number of other ways by bringing the unemployed persons together with the employers.

276. In order to be eligible for labour mediation, the interested party has to register with the National Employment Administration and submit information about himself/herself relevant to mediation.[229] Also, as stipulated by the Act (Articles 45–46), the Administration is bound to make an 'individual employment plan' with each unemployed person within a period of ninety days. This plan has to envisage actual steps to be taken in ensuring a job to the unemployed person, and it has to be updated at six months intervals. In making these plans, priority is given to 'less employable persons' – the category of persons who are expected to meet greater difficulties in their search for new job owing to their poor health, insufficient or inadequate education, socio-demographic characteristics, regional or occupational discrepancy between the offer and demand on the existing labour market, and other objective reasons.[230]

277. When an employer reports to the Administration the need for qualified staff, the Administration has to forward this information about the opening, conditions and deadline to apply to the unemployed and those seeking a change of jobs immediately. For such purposes, the Administration can make a pre-selection of candidates.

278. At the request of the unemployed person or employer, the Administration can also help with job applications or with other documents connected with the employment process.[231] The costs of mailing the application can also be covered if the unemployed person is receiving minimum income benefits (*see* further). The costs of public transportation to the interview can be covered as well if the offered job happens to be outside the place of person's residence. If such persons get employment outside their place of residence, they are entitled to a compensation that covers their travelling expenses and moving.[232]

279. The Administration also helps employers find candidates for short-term employment or for some other types of flexible hours of work (temporary employment, part-time work).

280. Certain categories of persons are prioritized for labour mediation (persons who are expected to meet greater difficulties in their search for a new job – *see* above). The unemployed persons experiencing greater difficulties in finding employment are aided by the basic proactive measures of employment policy and receive priority treatment through intensified measures of employment policy

229. *See* Arts 85–90 of the Act on Employment and Insurance against Unemployment.
230. *See* Art. 31 of the Act on Employment and Insurance against Unemployment.
231. *See* Art. 9 of the Act on Employment and Insurance against Unemployment.
232. *See* Art. 31 para. 2 of the Act on Employment and Insurance against Unemployment.

defined by the Ministry. These are primarily invalids and other handicapped individuals, as well as some other categories of unemployed persons who find it more difficult to find a new job.[233]

281. To promote labour mediation, the Administration also helps the employers in a number of following ways:

- by analysing current situation and monitoring fluctuation on the labour market;
- by organizing group and individual talks with unemployed persons;
- by making a selection of candidates;
- by assisting in creation of programmes and by establishing measures that will solve the problem of surplus workers (and in defining criteria for redundant workers);
- by offering an expert help in additional education and training, etc.

282. For labour mediation to be successful, another entitlement is significant – 'information on the possibilities and conditions of employment'. The right to be informed is exercised through local employment services, which are obliged to post new openings on the bulletin board, on the Website of the National Employment Administration within twenty-four hours or in the newspaper of the Administration.[234]

283. Since the process of economic restructuring and privatization is expected to result in a significant labour surplus, some new mechanisms of labour mediation were introduced in 2002 – the 'Employment and Professional Orientation Exhibition' (recently named as 'employment exhibition', 'professional orientation fair', and 'education fair') and the 'Job Hunting Club'. An employment exhibition can be organized on a municipal or provincial level to provide unemployed persons with an opportunity of demonstrating their skills and knowledge to interested employers. The job-hunting clubs should offer the unemployed a possibility of learning new skills and becoming educated and trained in relevant fields, so that they can actively pursue employment. Additionally, the club is supposed to provide information about new openings, offer individual and group counselling, and provide expert help and advice in confidence building and help in finding employment.[235]

§2. Vocational Training

284. One of the rights of unemployed persons in accordance with Serbian legislation is the right to 'additional education and training'. This right is aimed at enabling the unemployed as well as to redundant workers to continue learning and

---

233. In the case of hiring such a person, the employer acquires right to pay lower contributions (*see* above). *See also* Arts 15, 35, 73, 87, 94 of the Regulation on the Criteria and Ways of Implementation of Proactive Measures of Employment Policy.
234. *See* Arts 6, 20 of the Act on Employment and Insurance against Unemployment.
235. *See* Arts 13 and 19–20 of the Regulation on the Criteria and Ways of Implementation of Proactive Measures of Employment Policy.

developing new skills, to change their occupational status in order to easily find employment. In accordance with Article 52 of the Employment Act, additional education and training include theoretical and practical education aimed at acquiring new techniques and skills to raise the possibility of employment or self-employment.

285. The goal of vocational training is to increase 'employability' of persons encountering difficulties in finding new jobs, either because of the oversupply/inadequacy of their professional knowledge and skills at the labour market. Special attention is given to freshmen and apprentices.

286. Unemployed persons registered with the National Employment Administration are obliged to accept and successfully complete the education and training programmes that have been recommended by the Fund. These programmes are organized by either the Administration or the employers (e.g., for training of redundant workers). If the vocational training has been initiated by the employers, they also have to cover the costs, whereas in other cases it is financed from the insurance fund. In addition to paid education and training (transport, manuals), the unemployed person is at the same time entitled to unemployment benefits. There is also a possibility to have the cost of such training covered by the Administration at the request of the employer, in which case the employer undertakes the obligation to employ persons who have successfully completed the training.[236]

287. The rights and obligations binding the National Employment Administration, the training participants, educational and other relevant organizations, are regulated by a contract. If an unemployed person, having completed vocational training, refuses employment, abandons training without a justified reason or becomes expelled from training by his/her own fault, the person is under the obligation to reimburse the costs. If the training is interrupted because of the employer, the employer is obliged to reimburse the Fund for the costs of preparatory activities and the expenses related to financial aid.

§3. Direct Work Provision

288. The direct work provision is, at present, not highly developed in Serbia, due to insufficient State funds allocated for these purposes. However, furnishing subsidies for work provision by the National Employment Administration is becoming a frequent practice.

289. One type of direct provision of work is conducted by means of receiving education and training for (and by) a known employer (*see* above). Assistance in self-employment falls indirectly under this category and entails providing a single

236. *See* Arts 52–55 of the Act on Employment and Insurance against Unemployment and Arts 49–86 the Regulation on the Criteria and Ways of Implementation of Proactive Measures of Employment Policy.

unemployment benefit payment to the unemployed or furnishing subsidies for opening private shops or companies.[237] Accordingly, Article 51 of the Act on Employment and Insurance against Unemployment assistance in self-employment anticipates subsidies or expert help and counselling to an unemployed person or group of persons wishing to open a shop, set up a cooperative business, a farm, agricultural holding or any other form of entrepreneurship including business association/company. One of the preconditions to be fulfilled before receiving a subsidy is successful completion of training in entrepreneurship, organized by the National Employment Administration.[238]Also, one type of direct work provision provides Article 50 of the Act on Employment, which anticipates subsidies granted to employers for opening new posts that are intended for unemployed and less employable persons.

290. Subsidies cover wages for newly employed workers during a limited period of time.[239] Also, subsidies are used to cover social insurance contributions for the period of twenty-four to twenty-six months, as anticipated by the Act on Contributions for Obligatory Social Insurance (*see* above).

291. The Employment Act also anticipates the possibility of temporary employment for the unemployed at public works (in social, humanitarian, cultural activities and other jobs of general interest; at maintaining and rebuilding the infrastructure, and environmental protection). In accordance with Article 58 of the Act, the priority in hiring persons for public works is given to less employable and poor unemployed persons. Public works are conducted by the employer chosen in open public competition declared by the National Employment Administration.[240]

237. *See* Arts 51 and 74 of the Act on Employment and Insurance against Unemployment and Arts 42–48 the Regulation on the Criteria and Ways of Implementation of Proactive Measures of Employment Policy.
238. *See* Arts 41 and 43 of the Regulation on the Criteria and Ways of Implementation of Proactive Measures of Employment Policy.
239. *See* Arts 29–38 of the Regulation on the Criteria and Ways of Implementation of Proactive Measures of Employment Policy.
240. *See* Arts 94–101 of the Regulation on the Criteria and Ways of Implementation of Proactive Measures of Employment Policy.

Chapter 2. Unemployment Benefit

§1. Field of Application

I. Territorial

292. The unemployment insurance system in Serbia is set up so that it provides protection for insured persons who used to work within the territory of the State and whose employers are registered within its territory. As an exception, the insurance is also extended to cover détaché (posted) workers unless they are insured abroad.

II. Personal

293. Regarding personal coverage, unemployment insurance is extremely comprehensive. It encompasses not only wage earners, but also public-sector employees, State officials, self-employed persons (including both founders and co-founders of commercial enterprises), as well as persons performing temporary and occasional work. Also, no difference is drawn between those permanently employed and those working on short-term contracts. Only independent agricultural workers (farmers) have remained outside of this system. Like other uninsured persons, they can get insured on a voluntary basis.

§2. Amount of the Benefit

294. The way of calculating financial compensation was changed at the end of 2017 and now it is similar to calculating pensions. The monthly amount of the compensation represents the combination of two elements: (1) daily financial compensation and (2) the number of (calendar) days in a month for which the right is granted and the payment is made. Daily financial compensation also consists of two elements. It is established by multiplying the basis for daily financial compensation by personal coefficient. Personal coefficient represents the relation of gross income, that is, the compensation of income, the insurance basis and the amount of stipulated compensation over the past twelve months preceding the termination of employment contract and insurance and average yearly income per employed paid in the RS according to the latest publicized statistical data provided by the relevant government agency.[241]

295. A minimum and maximum limits of the benefit have also been set. They are established in nominal amount in accordance to the Law. The benefit cannot be set below RSD 22,390 (about EUR 189), and it cannot exceed RSD 51,905 (about

241. *See* Art. 69 of the Act on Employment and Insurance against Unemployment.

EUR 440). Once a year these limits are harmonized with the yearly index of consumer prices over the calendar year which precedes the year in which harmonization is established. The bases for compensation are harmonized in the same way. Also, the Act on Employment and Insurance against Unemployment (Article 55) stipulates 'Stimulation for beneficiaries of unemployment benefit'. If the beneficiary of the benefit manages to find permanent employment after three months from the date of getting the right to the benefit, he/she will receive 30% of the overall benefit (without social security contributions) as an incentive.

296. The duration of the compensation payments is dependent on the number of years the beneficiary paid contributions. The unemployment benefit is paid from three months (for a length of service of five years) to twenty-four months (if the person needs only two years to achieve an old-age pension).[242]

297. The unemployment benefit is paid at the end of each month (for the previous month). At the request of the unemployed person, it can also be paid in a lump-sum provided that these resources are used for entrepreneurial purposes (*see* above).

298. If the unemployed person's right to unemployment benefit ends earlier, when reassessing the person's entitlement, the insurance coverage prior to the last instalment will not be added into the calculation.[243]

§3. Conditions

299. To avoid the possibility of abuse of this benefit, legislation has imposed numerous eligibility conditions and restrictions.

300. The first condition is that the unemployed person, prior to the termination of work, has completed a certain number of days of work. It is necessary that the unemployed person had mandatory insurance for at least twelve months, or eighteen months with interruptions (interruptions up to thirty days are not considered to interfere with the continuity of insurance) prior to applying for unemployment benefit.

301. Some periods of inactivity are included to periods of work, so that benefit payments continue throughout the following periods:

– while the unemployed person is undergoing further education and training;

---

242. Until 17 May 2001, senior workers were entitled to special protection. Persons insured for thirty and over thirty years had the right to compensation until they found new employment or fulfilled requirements for pension. However, due to the chronic financial crisis, this privilege was revoked. Re-introduction of this privilege is being considered again since it became obvious that senior workers experience great difficulties in finding new jobs.

243. *See* Arts 66–77 of the Act on Employment and Insurance against Unemployment.

- of temporary incapacity to work as determined in accordance with health insurance regulations, for as long as the incapacity lasts;
- of maternity leave, childcare leave and special childcare leave.

302. The second group of conditions relates to formally achieving the status of an unemployed person. In order for somebody to become registered as unemployed, in accordance with Article 2 of the Act, it is required that:

- the person is between the ages of 15 and 65 years;
- that the person is capable and ready to start working immediately;
- that the person has not entered into employment elsewhere or otherwise exercised their right to work;
- that the person is actively seeking employment.

Full-time students (until the age of 26), a person who met requirements needed for retirement, a person whose rights from work have been suspended, as determined by labour law (i.e., a person whose labour relation has been temporarily suspended during his service in the Army, sent abroad, performing duties for the State, etc.),[244] cannot be categorized as unemployed entitled to unemployment benefits.

303. The third group of conditions concerns the method of termination of employment. In accordance with Article 67 of the Employment Act, the unemployment benefit is due only to individuals whose grounds of mandatory insurance did not end through their own wish or fault (the Act precisely stipulates reasons for justified termination of employment).

304. The right to unemployment benefits, as well as other entitlements included in unemployment insurance, is realized on the basis of a request. Timely filing of this request is the fourth important condition for eligibility for unemployment benefits. The interested party has to submit the request within thirty days of the termination of contract. In that case, payments will be made starting with the first day of unemployment. If the request is submitted late, the compensation will be paid only for the time left, and if it is submitted after the cut-off date, the person will lose the right to unemployment benefits. These deadlines will not be applicable if the person was incapacitated to work in accordance with health insurance regulations (*see* above).[245]

305. The request for benefit payments should be submitted to the organizational unit of the National Employment Administration based on the place of residence or the place of termination of employment. The first instance of decision-making about

244. *See* Art. 79 of the Act on Labour.
245. *See* Art. 68 of the Act on Employment and Insurance against Unemployment.

the request is made by the branch office, that is, its manager. The head office, that is, the Director of the National Employment Administration, makes rulings on appeals.[246]

306. In order to avoid the abuse of benefits, unemployment beneficiaries are obliged to report to the Administration every thirty days, as well as to respond to each inquiry. In addition, the beneficiary has to inform the Administration of every change in status within five days. If the unemployed person fails to report new facts that may lead to a suspension or revocation of rights, or if it is determined that the right was realized on the bases of false data, the unemployed will be obliged to return the full amount of payments already made.

307. The individuals will be deprived of their right to unemployment benefits:

– if they are no longer considered as unemployed;
– if they are removed from the Administration List of unemployed persons;[247]
– refuse suitable employment;[248]
– fail to inform the Administration of every change in status within five days;
– if he/she is working without employment contract (unreported employment).

308. If the person enjoying unemployment benefits starts working part-time, joins the army, ends up in prison or similar institution for the period up to six months, goes abroad or is sent abroad together with his/her spouse on governmental assignment, the right to unemployment benefit will be temporary suspended.[249]

---

246. *See* Art. 80 of the Act on Employment and Insurance against Unemployment and Arts 35–37 of the Statute of the National Employment Administration, of 15 Jan. 2010.
247. *See* Arts 76 and 87–88 of the Act on Employment and Insurance against Unemployment.
248. What is considered to be a suitable employment depends on the duration of the state of unemployment. For the first twelve months of unemployment, it is employment at the same level, qualifications and type of job, whereas after that period, it is employment at the lower level of the same qualifications and type of job. *See* Art. 33 of the Act on Employment and Insurance against Unemployment.
249. *See* Art. 75 of the Act on Employment and Insurance against Unemployment.

Part VIII. Pensions

309. The pension system in Serbia provides the working population and their family members with protection against negative effects that often accompany old age, death, and the incapacity to work. Parallel to these three risks are three types of pensions: old age, family and invalidity (disability). This part of the monograph will deal with old-age and family pensions.

310. The pension system in Serbia mainly operates completely under the auspices (control) of the State. Private pension systems have just started to evolve (*see* above). The pension system is financed on the principle of 'pay-as-you-go', that is, pensions are paid from the contributions being made by the current working population.

311. One of the common features of the pension system is that pension regulations for all employed persons are almost identical. Because of this, wage earners, public-sector employees and the self-employed are legally treated in the same manner. The only differences pertain to the method of calculating contributions (different contribution bases), which in reality leads to considerable differences in pension amounts. As a rule, they are lower for self-employed persons, especially for agricultural workers.

312. All administrative activities relating to pensions are conducted by one institution – the Republic Fund for Pension and Disability Insurance. Contributed assets for employees, self-employed persons and agricultural workers (farmers) were managed as separate funds until 2011, and thereafter, they are consolidated.

Chapter 1. Pensions for Wage Earners

313. The pension system for wage earners encompasses public-sector pensions as well. The same type of insurance also covers employees engaged in exhausting or particularly dangerous jobs – such as the army, police, corrections workers, coalminers, seamen, with the reservation that certain special rules apply to these groups. This insurance provides the insurers with old-age and survivors' pensions, as well as with disability pensions (*see* above).

314. Persons not protected under a State pension scheme have the right to voluntarily participate in the State pension insurance system. Additionally, voluntary pension insurance that can be provided both by State funds and private institutions is also allowed. On 6 October 2005, the Act on Voluntary Pension Funds and Pension Plans was adopted.[250] Voluntary pension funds are functioning as independent financial institutions that collect and invest pension contributions into different assets in order to increase the value of financial resources gathered in this way, with a minimum of investment risk. Services provided by these funds are financed from collected contributions (3%) and from annual remuneration/payment for these services (1.25% of total assets of a voluntary pension fund). Assets of each insured person are kept on a separate account. All information related to the data on personal accounts has to be available to the insured person at all times. Financial resources on these accounts could be transferred to another pension fund at the request of the insured person at any time. Operation of private pension funds is controlled by the National Bank of Serbia.[251]

§1. Old-Age Pension

I. Beneficiaries

A. Territorial Field of Application

315. The system of old-age pension beneficiaries in Serbia is regulated in the same way as the system of payment contributions for pensions (*see* above). That is to say, entitlement to pensions pertains mainly to persons who legally work within the territory of the State. This may be both foreigners as well as individuals without citizenship. Pension insurance also covers détaché (posted) workers and uninsured domestic citizens working abroad, as well as those individuals who cannot enjoy these benefits outside the foreign country.

250. Official Herald of the RS, Nos 85/2005, 31/2011. The new Serbian Act on pensions of (NE: on) 2003 anticipated the adoption of a special Act on Voluntary Pension and Disability Insurance (Art. 16 of the Act on Pension and Disability Insurance). On 1 Jul. 2011, the Regulation on Conditions, Organizing Procedures and Functioning of Private Pension Plans was adopted (Official Herald of the RS, No. 48/2011). *See* also: *Propisi iz oblasti poslova nadzora dobrovoljnih penzijskih fondova (Regulations in the field of supervision of voluntary pension funds)*, Narodna banka Srbije (National Bank of Serbia), https://www.nbs.rs/internet/latinica/20/index_npf.html.
251. *See* Arts 3, 23, 31, 41, 44 and 68 of the Act on Voluntary Pension Funds and Pension Plans.

316. As far as pension payments are concerned, they are primarily paid on the territory of the State. Payments abroad are possible if so specified by international (bilateral) agreements or on the condition of reciprocity. The same is true for foreign citizens and individuals without citizenship who have fulfilled the requirements for pension in Serbia, but who live abroad.[252]

317. The collapse of the SFRY created a specific problem concerning pension payments. A large number of individuals who had been enjoying their pension benefits from the countries that seceded from SFRY found themselves without income within the former FRY. For these persons – now refugees – a Federal Act adopted in 1996 allowed them the option of temporary payments by a host country in the case where they were not in a position to receive a pension where they had originally earned it. The same provision existed in the Act on Pension Insurance of Serbia (Article 256).[253] This issue has been generally settled by bilateral agreements between ex-Yugoslav Republics, today independent States (*see* above).

B. Personal Field of Application

318. The personal field of application of the pension system corresponds to the contribution obligation. This means that primary insurance covers wage earners (and self-employed persons). However, there is an extension within the field of application due to the inclusion of certain periods of inactivity, covered by other social benefits, into the periods of work. In such cases, contributions are paid by other social security insurance institutions.

319. In order to be entitled to a pension in Serbia, the relevant insurance period that is taken into account is officially referred to as the 'contribution period'. The 'contribution period' can be divided as follows:

- 'term of employment' (which can be of two types – 'term of employment at actual duration' and 'term of employment at an accelerated rate' (for persons with shortened period of service); and
- '*special term of employment*'.

320. Term of employment at actual duration represents the basic type of length of service, which, as a rule, corresponds to the period spent as an employee or as self-employed. In addition, the rights relating to this type also cover persons who for various reasons lost their jobs, and thereby pension insurance, but for whom specific conditions permit the continuation of contribution payments. The following persons may be entitled to this so-called extended insurance:

- those on professional development or specialization or vocational re-training;

252. In practice, pension payments abroad are approved for all interested individuals, that is, the reciprocity rule is not strictly abided by. *See* Art. 124 of the Act on Pension and Disability Insurance.
253. This Article was, in the meantime, removed from the Act.

- those receiving an unemployment allowance;
- participants in lawful strikes;
- persons on temporary or occasional employment outside the company;
- self-employed persons temporarily not working, but with settled due contributions;
- those who paid contributions after the termination of mandatory insurance.

321. Beside the contribution period that comes from the length of employment, there is also a 'special term of employment'. Special term of employment represents compensation by the State for the fact that a person's specific circumstances had prevented him/her from working. Such persons are entitled to a special term of employment despite the fact that they had not been paying contributions. According to former federal legislation, the right to a special term of employment covered veterans and prisoners of war from the wars fought on the territory of Yugoslavia in the last century. For example, veterans from the wars of the late 1990s got the time spent at the war front calculated into the special term of employment at a double rate.[254] Persons who were wounded or became sick during the war got the period spent undergoing treatment and rehabilitation calculated into the special term of employment. Additionally, another basis for the special term of employment in Serbia was introduced for the purpose of stimulating the birth rate. A woman who gives birth to a third child gets two bonus years calculated into her regular term of employment. Also, an insured person, in particular a woman who gives birth to a child, is entitled to a special term of employment as follows: six months (if she gives birth to one child); one year (if she gives birth to two children).[255]

II. Conditions

322. In Serbia, the concept of the flexible retirement age applies. This simply means that old-age pension is possible at different stages of life, which, for standard categories of insured persons, falls between the ages of 58 and 65.[256]

323. The conditions for old-age pension are equal for all regardless of status (wage earners, public employees, or self-employed). Differences are based on the length of the contribution period and gender (women are allowed to retire earlier than men). As of 2014, a category of an 'early retirement' was introduced to facilitate the possibility of obtaining the status of a retired person earlier than anticipated

254. Conditions for this have been specified by the special Act on the Yugoslav Army of 27 May 1994 (Official Gazette of the FRY, Nos 43/1994, 44/1999, 74/1999, 3/ 2002, 37/2002).
255. This regulation is not going to be implemented before 2032. *See* Art. 60 of the Act on Pension and Disability Insurance.
256. In fact, in 2019 men can take early retirement when they are at least 57 years and 8 months of age. In accordance with Art. 175 of the Act on Labour of Serbia, the employee is entitled to work longer if so agreed with the employer, as long as he/she has the 'capacity to work'.

by the regular rules and conditions. In such a case, however, the pension is permanently decreased.[257] The right to old-age pension covers persons who meet some of the following requirements:

- if they turn 65 (men) or 62 years and 6 months (women – in 2019) and have at least a fifteen-year contribution period;[258]
- any age if they have forty-five years of contribution period;
- if they have forty years of insurance contributions and are at least 60 years of age (so-called early retirement pension).[259]

324. Some occupations allow for shorter careers, because the years of insurance are calculated at an accelerated rate. This includes persons who work in extremely difficult and dangerous fields and jobs hazardous to health (such as jobs with the army, police, tax police, prisons, mines) or such jobs that cannot be performed with the same success at all ages (e.g., opera singers, ballet dancers). Their length of service can be calculated with an acceleration of up to 50%, meaning that if such a person were to work effectively for twelve months, the length of service would be counted as eighteen months. Additionally, for this category of employees, the pensionable age-limit as prescribed above is lowered every few years (every three to six years of work, depending on the degree of increase of length of service) for work at difficult jobs, by one year. Thanks to this, they can retire earlier (but not before the age of 55, and 50 years of age only as an exception – for persons with an acceleration of 50%). The condition here is that they had spent at least two-thirds of their working life doing difficult jobs.[260]

325. Until December 1996 (which is when the former Act on Pension and Disability Insurance was adopted),[261] there existed another option to shorten 'pension careers' in Serbia. It was possible to buy service years so that they would add up to retirement eligibility; this was applied to older employees who had been laid off without having reached retirement age. Their employers could pay for up to five years of pension contributions. Due to the rapid increase in the number of pensioners, which became overly burdensome to the pensions funds, buying length of service years was suspended.

257. This pension was introduced by the Amendments to the Act on Pension and Disability Insurance, of 21 Jul. 2014 (Official Herald of the RS, No. 75/2014).
258. According to the said amendments of July 2014, this requirement will be gradually increased each year until 2032. It is anticipated that by that time women and men alike will, when retiring, have to meet the same age requirement (65 years of age).
259. Early retirement pension is reduced by 0.34% for each year of retiring before the age of 65. Maximum total reduction can amount up to 20.4%. Besides, until the year of 2024, early retirement will be allowed, to some extent, even before the said age. Regulations are, however, growing more severe each year. This, in particular, means that in 2019 men can obtain early retirement if they have worked for forty years and are 57 years and 8 months old while for women it is thirty-eight years and six months of work and 57 years of age. *See* Arts 19b, 19v, 70 a, b, of the Amendments on Act on Pension and Disability Insurance.
260. Article 20 of the Act on Pension and Disability Insurance stipulates that the age-limit for the category in question may be lowered to 50 years (for employees doing most difficult jobs).
261. Official Herald of the RS, Nos 52/1996, 46/1998, 29/2001.

III. Pension Calculation

326. The primary criterion for determining the amount of old-age pension in Serbia is the level of investment in pension funds. It is evaluated based on two elements:

(1) career duration; and
(2) earnings of the employee in that period, that is, level of contribution payments.

327. Family status has no influence on the amount of old-age pension, but the sex of the insured person does (women are entitled to an increase in the calculation of their contribution period for a career but men are not).[262]

328. The Act on Pension and Disability Insurance of 2003 has introduced radical changes in pension calculation. It aims to tie pension amounts to the insured person's total investments into the funds, as well as to encourage the insured to focus more on the amounts and continuity of investments. This has been achieved by changing the method of pension calculation: it is no longer calculated on the basis of the ten most lucrative years of one's career, but rather on the basis of contribution payments throughout one's career.

329. Pension calculation, according to the new legislation, is very complex, but it was developed with the intention of making sure that the pension amounts really correspond to actual investments in pension funds. The pension amount is calculated by multiplying the insured person's 'personal points' with the 'general point' at its value on the day of reaching pension eligibility (Articles 61–64). Whereas, a 'personal point' is the figure resulting from multiplying the insured person's 'personal quotient' with his/her contribution period. The 'personal quotient' is determined for each separate year of work by calculating the ratio between the annual (gross or net) earnings and the average salary in the Republic for that particular year. 'Earnings' cover all other types of income the insured person made in that year based on his/her work, provided that the earnings were the basis for contributions. This includes compensation on the grounds of health insurance and during maternity leave.

330. Only contribution periods of up to forty-five years are taken into consideration.[263] Women are in a better position regarding pension calculation because their contribution period is increased by a bonus of 8% (in 2019).[264] The right to such a shortened length of service applies also to disabled workers under specific

262. According to Art. 69, para. 1 of the Act on Pension and Disability Insurance, if meeting the said age requirement, a women pensioner will receive an increase of 6%.
263. *See* Art. 68 of the Act on Pension and Disability Insurance of Serbia. Calculations take proportionately into account contribution periods shorter than a year.
264. According to the aforementioned amendments to the Act of 2010, that bonus will be reduced by 1% each year until 2023 when it is planned to reach the level of 6%.

conditions (*see* above). The right to a 20% higher pension applies also to a number of insured persons whose contribution period falls under the category of shortened length of service (police staff and services related to State security, some categories of prison staff, Foreign Ministry staff and tax police staff).[265]

331. The second element in the pension calculation equation – 'the general point' – is determined on the basis of all pensions and personal points of those old-age and disability pension beneficiaries who became entitled to a pension between 1 January 2001 and 30 June 2002. The determined 'general point' is then adjusted in the same way as pensions (*see* further) (Article 70).

332. Since the average pension is very low in comparison to the cost of living, the law has determined a threshold pension that should guarantee a minimum for survival. The pension cannot be lower than 27% of the average salary within the territory of the Republic in the preceding year. In order for the pension funds to protect themselves from excessive expenses, a pension ceiling has been introduced. This was determined by limiting the 'personal quotient' by means of allowing it to be 3.8 at the most.[266] The highest pension, in the amount of RSD 132,065 (about EUR 1,111) in 2019, has been received by only twenty-five pensioners (out of slightly over 1.7 million). At the same time, 105,000 pensioners have received the lowest pension which amounts up to RSD 10,000 (about EUR 85) which means that the lowest pension is thirteen times lower than the highest.[267]

333. In order to preserve pensioners' living standards, an occasional pension adjustment is anticipated. For a number of years, pensions used to be adjusted against average salary fluctuations. However, it became evident that this method did not sufficiently take into account the overall state of the economy in the country. Since the 2003 Act on Pension and Disability Insurance (Article 80), all pensions were adjusted on every 1 April and 1 October according to the cost of living in the six preceding months. From 2011, all pensions will be adjusted according to fluctuations in consumers' prices.[268] As mentioned before, since 2014, legal regulations

265. An entitlement to such increase is not granted to persons performing administrative – technical jobs in the said professions. It only applies to persons performing exceptionally hard, hazardous or potentially health damaging work as well as those persons who would not be capable of performing such work after they have reached a certain age. *See* Arts 42 and 79 of the Act on Pension and Disability Insurance.

266. *See* Arts 76 and 78 of the Act on Pension and Disability Insurance.

267. *Najviša penzija u Srbiji iznosi 132.000 dinara, evo koliko penzionera mesečno prima toliko (The highest Pension in Serbia is 132,000 Dinars, Here's How Many Pensioners Receive So Much per Month)*, 'Blic' (daily newspaper), 29 May 2019, https://www.blic.rs/vesti/drustvo/najvisa-penzija-u-srbiji-iznosi-132000-dinara-evo-koliko-penzionera-mesecno-prima/chpy734.

268. Exceptionally, if the gross national product in the previous calendar year rises more than 4%, then the pensions are adjusted from 1 April of the current year according to the percentage obtained from consumer price index rates and gross product. *See* Art. 80 of the Act on Pension and Disability Insurance.

on harmonizing have been suspended. Since then the pensions have been harmonized in the way which is regulated by the acts applied to administering the budget system and only if it is estimated that the pension budget will take no more than 11% of GDP (*see* above).

334. Administrative rules governing admission, calculation and payment of all types of pensions are based on a special kind of administrative procedure called a 'general administrative proceeding'. This procedure consists of procedural rules that are binding to all State bodies when they make decisions pertaining to citizens' rights.[269] Proceedings related to pensions are under the jurisdiction of those branch offices of the Pension and Disability Insurance Fund where the insured person was either originally insured or where he/she completed the major portion of his/her contribution period. The institution is obliged to provide the insured with expert help if needed.

335. If insured persons are not satisfied with the ruling by the Pension and Disability Fund Insurance, they may appeal within fifteen days upon receiving the ruling to an appellate body within the Fund. After that they can appear before the court where such cases are handled in a specific procedure called an administrative dispute, before the Administrative Court. As an exception, after the expiration of court protection deadlines, there is the possibility of retrial before the social insurance institution. This option is possible if new facts or evidence surface that could lead to a different outcome in the case.[270]

336. Pension payments begin from the day a person fulfils the pension requirements.[271] If the application for pension is submitted after the deadline, payments can be made only six months retroactively. Pension payments should be conducted once a month for the preceding month, at the place of residence of the insurer. However, in reality it has been the case that pensions were over a year late (for instance, in 2000).

337. Regarding the possibilities of post-retirement work, the Serbian old-age pensions are actually something in between a true old-age pension and a retirement pension. In fact, in order to increase employment, it is expected that a person who retires does not work anymore. But a retired person in Serbia is allowed to apply for another job or to continue private businesses (without revoking or reducing pensions). Nor are there any limitations related to so-called permitted employment, which exist in some countries. The retired person is, of course, obliged to make all contribution payments for social insurance like every other employee. This is why

269. *See* the Act on General Administrative Procedure, of 1 Mar. 2016 (Official Herald of the RS, Nos 18/2016 i 95/2018).
270. *See* Arts 99, 103 and 104 of the Act on Pension and Disability Insurance.
271. According to Art. 120 of the Act, those beneficiaries who pay the pension and disability contributions on their own and have failed to cover the entire due contribution period will be entitled to the rights arising from the pension and disability insurance in proportion to periods for which the contribution was paid.

retired people are entitled to a re-assessment of their pensions once they stop working. The option of reactivation does not apply if the person finds employment or works as self-employed abroad.[272]

338. Certain social security branches regulations stipulate strict accumulation rules so as not to duplicate benefits. Old-age pension cannot be accompanied with other uncomplimentary social benefits (such as benefits from unemployment insurance, minimum income benefit, invalid or survivors' pension).[273] But having a State pension does not exclude the right to receive part of the pension from abroad or from private pension funds.

§2. Survivors' Pension

339. The goal of survivors' pension is to ensure the essential needs of the insured person's surviving dependents. This is why the conditions for entitlement to this kind of pension are different from those governing old-age pensions.

I. Beneficiaries

340. The right to a survivor's pension covers family members of the insured person, that is, the person enjoying some of the benefits from his/her pension-disability insurance (old-age pension, disability pension) which includes:

- spouse (including divorced spouse if he/she meets the requirements of being supported);
- children – marital, born out of wedlock, adopted;
- step-children, grandchildren, brothers, sisters and other children without parents or children whose parents are incapacitated to work, whom the deceased used to support;
- parents (father, mother, stepfather, stepmother, adoptive parents if the deceased used to support them).[274]

341. Status in the family can have an impact on the realization and the amount of pension. Spouses and children, adopted children, step-children and grandchildren are considered members of the immediate family. Parents, siblings and other children that used to be supported by the deceased are considered members of the extended family.

---

272. *See* Art. 121 of the Act on Pension and Disability Insurance.
273. *See* Art. 119 of the Act on Pension and Disability Insurance.
274. In accordance with Art. 32 of the Act on Pension and Disability Insurance of Serbia, the deceased is considered to have supported a person if the total income per family head does not exceed the lowest pension in the previous quarter. The following are excluded from this rule: child allowance, birth grant, allowance for care and assistance, financial compensation for body injury, financial prize awards, severance pay due to retirement, and on the grounds of student standards.

II. Conditions

342. There are two sets of conditions that have to be satisfied in Serbia in order to qualify for a survivor's pension. First, there are certain requirements that have to be met by the deceased in order for the survivor's pension to be payable at all – these are so-called general conditions for survivor's pension. Second, there are also 'specific conditions' that have to be fulfilled by the heirs of the deceased.

343. In order for any family member to become entitled to survivor's pension, the deceased insured person needs to meet one of the so-called general conditions:

- that they have completed at least a five-year insurance period or that they have met the requirements for a disability pension;
- that they were an old-age or disability pension beneficiary.[275]

344. If the insured person's death was caused by an accident at work or a professional disease, the situation receives special treatment. In these cases, the family members become entitled to a survivor's pension regardless of the deceased person's contribution period.

345. 'Special conditions' take into account the social status, age and capacity to work of each category. At the same time priority is given to members of the immediate family, while members of the extended family are in a slightly less favourable position, meaning that they will become entitled to a pension only with the condition that the sum of the pensions of the members of the immediate family does not amount to the full amount of allowable pensionable earnings.

346. A widow becomes entitled to a survivor's pension if she:

- is 53 years old at the time of the death of the spouse;
- becomes completely incapacitated to work by the time of the death of the spouse or within a year of his death;
- one or more children entitled to survivor's pension is left in her care (if she becomes incapacitated to work during this time she retains the right to survivor's pension as long the condition lasts).

347. If a widow is younger than prescribed according to the above, yet older than 45 years, she will become entitled to a survivor's pension when she turns 53 years. Also, if the widow turns 45 years while exercising the right to a survivor's pension on the grounds of incapacity to work or parental duty, this right becomes permanent (if she is 45 years, she will have to wait for the pension until the age of 53 years). In the case that the widow has not become entitled to a pension or is waiting for one of the requirements to be fulfilled, Serbian legislation does not offer any kind of assistance (such as, for example, 'temporary benefit' that exists in some

275. In accordance with Art. 27 of the Act on Pension and Disability Insurance.

countries). She can only exercise her right to the minimum income benefit covered by social protection under the same conditions as other citizens (*see* further).

The length of the marriage has no impact on the pension, nor does the fact that a person remarries or not.

348. Conditions governing a widower's right to survivor's pension still reflect the traditional notion that the man is the breadwinner and should be the one to support his wife and children. In conformity with this, the widower becomes entitled to survivor's pension under less favourable conditions than those for women, if:

- he was 58 years old at the time of death of wife;
- he became incapacitated to work by the time of death of his wife or within a year of her death;
- one or more children entitled to a survivor's pension is left in his care (if he becomes incapacitated to work during this time, he retains the right to a survivor's pension as long the condition lasts);
- Similar to the rules that apply to widows, a widower who turns 58 years while receiving a survivor's pension becomes permanently entitled to it.[276]

349. A child is entitled to survivor's pension until the age of 15. If he/she is attending school, this right may be exercised as follows:

- until the age of 20, if they attend high-school;
- until the age of 26, if they attend university (until the age of 27 if they served in the army in the meantime);
- while incapable of living and working independently, and within the eligibility age for a survivor's pension;
- while incapable of living and working independently, after the eligibility age for a survivor's pension, but before the death of the insurer, provided that the insurer provided for the child until their death;[277]
- If a child's education was interrupted due to illness, the right to receive a pension will be extended to cover the period of illness accordingly.

350. A parent (father and mother, stepfather, stepmother and adoptive parent) who used to be supported by the deceased becomes entitled to survivor's pension if he/she:

- has turned 65 (men) or 60 (women);
- become permanently incapacitated to work.

276. From 2012, special treatment is to be given to the spouse of an army professional killed during military operations. He/she is entitled to family pension regardless of his/her actual age providing that he/she has not remarried or, in case he/she has children, the children have finished their schooling. *See* Art. 30a of the Act on Pension and Disability Insurance.

277. In addition, it is stipulated that an insurer's children with disability become entitled to survivor's pension regardless of when the incapacity to work began and whether it was employed prior to that.

III. Calculation

351. The method of calculating a survivor's pension is based on the old-age, early or disability pension due to the insured person at the time of his/her death, that is, on the pension he/she had been receiving. The pension amount depends on the number and status of dependants. If pension is due only to members of the immediate family or only to members of the extended family, it is determined according to the following percentages:

- for one member 70%;
- for two members 80%;
- for three members 90%;
- for four or more members 100%.[278]

352. In the case that both members of the immediate and extended family are entitled to the pension, members of the immediate family get their pension determined as described above, while members of the extended family are entitled only to the difference between the full amount and the part allocated for the immediate family. If both, the spouse and the divorced spouse prove to be entitled to a survivor's pension, the pension is set in the amount of one pension and then equally divided among the two parties.

353. Children who are left without both parents enjoy special protection. They are entitled to pensions from the other parent as well. In this case, the total amount cannot be higher than the maximum pensionable earnings.[279]

354. It is quite often the case that a survivor's pension is not sufficient for survival, especially if both immediate and extended family members are awarded. This is why a minimum has been prescribed by law. In Serbia, the lowest basis for determining a survivor's pension equals the deceased person's pension for a twenty-year contribution period.[280]

355. A survivor's pension is paid in one payment even when it is allocated for several persons, unless separate payments are specifically requested. If pension is due only for immediate family members or only extended family members who live in different households, it is divided equally. If the beneficiaries live in separate households and belong to different categories of kinship, the pension gets divided in proportion to their entitlements. If any of the beneficiaries cease to be entitled to the pension, the pension amount due to the other family members gets re-calculated (this does not apply if pension payments are temporarily stopped). There is also the

278. An entitlement to 100% survivor's pension is received also by the successors of a person who has a voluntary membership in compulsory pension insurance. *See* Art. 71 of the Act on Pension and Disability Insurance.
279. Articles 71 and 73 of the Act on Pension and Disability Insurance.
280. Article 72 of the Act on Pension and Disability Insurance.

possibility for the insured to become entitled to more types of pensions. In this case, a person is allowed to receive only one – the one of his/her own choosing.[281]

356. The law on pensions in Serbia also contains the option of revoking the right to a survivor's pension for a family member who is convicted of the insured person's death and who is at the same time the survivor's pension beneficiary.[282]

281. *See* Arts 116, 117 and 119 of the Act on Pension and Disability Insurance.
282. Article 118, para. 2 of the Act on Pension and Disability Insurance.

Chapter 2. Pensions for the Self-Employed

357. The rules governing pensions for the self-employed in Serbia are in essence the same as those that apply for wage earners because most issues are jointly regulated. This insurance also covers all persons who conduct business based on work by contract, and other such contracts that grant them compensation, and are not otherwise insured. This category, which used to be uninsured, has thereby been provided with the opportunity to enjoy pension and disability insurance rights.

§1. Old-Age Pensions

358. The only difference between the self-employed and other insured persons regarding old-age pension is the method in which pensionable earnings are determined. All other regulations on conditions, pension amounts, methods and payments are common. As a rule, the basis for self-employed persons' pension calculation in Serbia is the taxable profit or taxable income – for agricultural workers (*see* above).

§2. Survivors' Pension

359. Survivors' pension of self-employed persons in Serbia is in every aspect identical to wage earners' pension.

Chapter 3. Guaranteed Income for Old Persons

360. In Serbia, there is no special system of guaranteed income intended exclusively for old persons. They are provided for within the system of protection from poverty and established for the benefit of the overall population – social protection. In that sense, the elderly are treated equally with the rest of the population. Although age can be a factor when approving minimum income benefits and other social protection benefits (e.g., allowance for home care and assistance, placement in a social protection institution), the conditions for entitlement to these rights are primarily tied to the financial situation and capacity to work of the individual (*see* further).

Part IX. Handicapped Persons

361. There is no special branch of social security in Serbia dealing exclusively with benefits for handicapped persons. The protection of these individuals is provided within the framework of the general social protection system – social assistance – which is designed to protect every person who is not capable of providing means of existence for themselves. There is one more segment of social security that protects certain categories of handicapped persons. Specifically, just after World War II in the former Yugoslavia, a complex system for the protection of handicapped persons whose injury or illness happened as a result of war or military action was introduced, and this system still applies.

362. Benefits for the handicapped are provided for two reasons: the promotion of social integration of the handicapped and making their everyday lives easier. Serbian legislation contains numerous and very different benefits in this area, a detailed account of which would take up too much space here. Hence, we will present only the most significant benefits for the handicapped in greater detail. Also, we will not venture into details connected to the minimum income benefit of the handicapped because that branch of law represents only a segment of 'minimum income benefit', which is provided to all persons who for some reason do not have the means of providing an existence for themselves (*see* further).

363. Although the system of legal protection of the handicapped in Serbia seems comprehensive, in practice it does not function as efficiently as it should, due to a chronic lack of resources and widespread poverty in the country.[283] As a consequence, the social position of many handicapped persons is extremely poor.

283. *Bukvić: Ekstremno siromašnih u Srbiji pola miliona, žive sa 400 dinara dnevno (Bukvić: Extremely Poor in Serbia, Half a Million, Live on 400 Dinars a Day),* N1 (Television news portal), 4 Mar. 2019, http://rs.n1info.com/Biznis/a465193/Bukvic-Ekstremno-siromasnih-u-Srbiji-pola-miliona-zive-sa-400-dinara-dnevno.html. According to this Article 500,000 of Serbian citizens (out of a little fewer than 8,000,000) have a daily income of EUR 3.5.

Chapter 1. Social Integration

364. Fundamental and concrete rights related to social integration of invalids have been regulated by the Act on Professional Rehabilitation and Employment of Disabled Persons and the Act on Social Protection of 4 April 2011.[284] In addition, the Act on Prevention of Discrimination of Disabled Persons of 17 April 2006 should also enhance their social integration.[285] This Act prohibits discrimination of invalids in all areas of life, especially in connection to State and local administration regarding their association, use of public services and facilities, healthcare, education, employment, transportation, matrimonial and family relations. A disabled person exposed to discrimination is entitled to a court protection (elimination of discrimination and reimbursement), and the legal or physical entity that makes discrimination could even be fined (from RSD 10,000 to RSD 500,000 (EUR 125–EUR 6,250)).[286]

365. The Act on Professional Rehabilitation and Employment of Disabled Persons introduces fresh and more energetic concept of social integration of disabled persons. Among other things, the Act specifies that the employer has to employ one invalid person if he/she has more than twenty employees. The number of employed invalid persons rises with an increase in the overall number of employees.[287] If the employer fails to follow the instruction, he/she will be penalized by the State for each such person he/she failed to employ for the sum amounting to 50% of the average wage in the RS.[288] There are also some other incentive measures aimed at improving employment of disabled persons (such as: reimbursement for expenses incurred during the process of adapting the existing working place to the needs of the handicapped person, subsiding wages for the period of twelve months, setting up special companies for professional rehabilitation and employment of invalids, working centres for handicapped persons, 'social companies', etc.). Also, disabled persons are entitled to employment under special conditions and to rights based on proactive employment policy (*see* above).[289]

366. The aim of professional rehabilitation according to the Act on Professional Rehabilitation and Employment of Disabled Persons is to make the disabled persons employable, help them keep their present jobs and make progress in their careers. These activities are conducted by the National Employment Administration or special companies for professional rehabilitation and employment of invalids.[290]

---

284. The first Act is published in: Official Herald of the RS, Nos 36/2009, 32/2013 and the second in: Official Herald of the RS, No. 24/2011.
285. Official Herald of the RS, Nos 33/2006, 13/2016.
286. *See* Arts 43 and 46–52 of the Act on Prevention of Discrimination of Disabled Persons.
287. The employer with twenty to forty-nine employees has to employ one person with invalidity and one more for each fifty subsequent employees. *See* Art. 24 of the Act on Professional Rehabilitation and Employment of Disabled Persons.
288. *See* Arts 24–29 of the Act on Professional Rehabilitation and Employment of Disabled Persons.
289. *See* Arts 32, 34, 43, 45 of the Act on Professional Rehabilitation and Employment of Disabled Persons.
290. *See* Arts 12–21 of the Act on Professional Rehabilitation and Employment of Disabled Persons.

These companies can be set up by the State or its territorial units (a province, municipalities), business associations, associations of disabled persons or any other legal or physical entity. The only condition to be fulfilled is to have at least five invalid persons employed. Their work is financed from the national budget and from contributions paid by the employers for professional rehabilitation of disabled persons. Subsidies granted to them amount to 75% of the wage (including contributions for social security) for each disabled person employed, up to maximum of 50% of the average wage in Serbian economy. Professional rehabilitation of employees in these companies is financed by their employers if their disability was due to injury at work or occupational illness. At the same time, this is a way to motivate the employers in prevention of invalidity arising from work.[291]

367. The Act on Professional Rehabilitation and Employment of Disabled Persons provides for 'working centres' intended for long-term professional rehabilitation of disabled persons who are either incapable to work or achieve less than one-third of work efficiency in comparison to regular employees.[292] These centres, however, cannot be established by private entities/entrepreneurs. Working centres can be set up only by the State or by associations providing protection to disabled persons or organizations (or associations of their legal agents). A novelty in this domain are 'social companies or social organizations' set up with the aim to fulfil the needs of invalid persons. These companies and organizations have to employ at least one invalid person. Furthermore, a social company has an obligation to invest one part of its income into social integration and improvement of living and working conditions of disabled persons.[293]

368. The Act on Social Protection contains a few benefits that aim to promote social integration for the disabled persons. These are:

- services of assistance in independent living;
- the right to assistance in being trained for work;
- placement in a social protection institution.

369. Services of assistance in independent living include assistance at home, personal assistance, training needed for independent living and other kinds of assistance that facilitate active participation of invalid persons in social life. This entitlement is financed and organized by the municipality. It is provided to all persons who are not capable of taking care of themselves. It includes taking care of all necessary domestic tasks such as maintaining the household, purchasing food and other necessities, maintaining the personal hygiene of the handicapped person, and so on. While all the other above-mentioned rights are under the competence of the Republic, this entitlement is financed by the municipality. The municipality may request a

291. During professional rehabilitation, an invalid person is entitled to receive 100% of the average salary in the past three months preceding rehabilitation. If the person is unemployed, he/she receives 20% of the minimal wage in the Republic. *See* Arts 19–21 and 35–42 of the Act on Professional Rehabilitation and Employment of Disabled Persons.
292. *See* Arts 43–44 of the Act on Professional Rehabilitation and Employment of Disabled Persons.
293. *See* Art. 45 of the Act on Professional Rehabilitation and Employment of Disabled Persons.

contribution from the beneficiary and his/her relatives toward covering the costs stemming from this right. Decisions in this domain are ruled by the competent municipal administration.[294]

370. The right to assistance in becoming trained for work covers children and youth with developmental disabilities, as well as adults with disabilities who can be trained for work, provided that this right cannot be realized on any other grounds. These have to be persons who cannot receive an education, vocational re-training or get employed under normal conditions. The degree of the capability to work of the handicapped is estimated either in accordance with regulation on education or in accordance with the regulations on pension and disability insurance (*see* above).

371. The right to assisted training for work is actually a complex right encompassing several types of benefits:

- referrals for vocational development;
- financial security;
- compensation for the costs of accommodation at boarding-schools for pupils and students;
- transportation costs;
- compensation for the costs of training.

Compensation for costs of training includes several benefits as well:

- costs to equip the workplace where the handicapped person is to be trained;
- adjusting working conditions to the capabilities of the handicapped trainees;
- instructor's fees and other costs directly related to becoming trained for work.

372. As a rule, training for work is conducted in companies specializing in the training and employment of handicapped persons (work centres), and that are financed from the national budget. Upon the completion of training, the handicapped person starts employment under specific conditions (*see* above).[295]

373. The right to placement in a social protection institution refers to children (over 3 years of age) and disabled adults who are not capable of living independently with a family because of unfavourable health, social, housing or family problems. In addition to being provided with housing, medical care and meals, these persons are also trained to perform certain jobs; they undergo rehabilitation programmes or become engaged in jobs that are suitable to their capabilities to work.[296]

294. Article 45 of the Act on Social Protection.
295. *See* Arts 108–109 and Art. 61 of the Act on Social Protection.
296. *See* Arts 51–54 of the Act on Social Protection.

374. In addition to the cited rights, which are valid for all handicapped persons, there are also three categories of war or military invalids that have numerous additional rights aimed at their social integration. These are:

- disabled veterans;
- peacetime military invalids;
- civilian war invalids (*see* further).

375. In accordance with the former Federal Act on the Basic Rights of Soldiers, Soldiers with Disabilities and the Families of Soldiers Killed at War of 15 May 1998 (which still applies in Serbia),[297] the rights of these persons aimed at their integration into society are:

- care and assistance allowance;
- the right to orthopaedic and other auxiliary devices;
- spa treatments and treatments involving a change of climate;
- free or subsidized use of public transportation;
- the right to a motor vehicle.

Each of these rights has special conditions attached, primarily to do with the degree of invalidity, but additional conditions such as capacity to work, age and financial situation are all taken into account as well.

376. Additionally, military and war invalids have certain rights specified in the Act on the Rights of Veterans, Military Invalids and Members of their Families adopted in Serbia on 25 November 1989.[298] These are:

- the right to compensation for the costs of placement in a social protection institution;
- the right to professional rehabilitation and a financial allowance during professional rehabilitation;
- the right to compensation for transportation costs incurred while receiving treatment.

297. Official Gazette of the FRY, Nos 24/1998, 29/98, 25/2000; and Official Herald of the RS, Nos 101/20005, 111/2009, 50/2018.

298. The Act was published in the Official Herald of the RS, Nos 54/1989, 137/2004, 50/2018. The Government of Serbia has drawn up a draft of a new Act/Law on the Rights of Veterans, Military Invalids, Civil Invalids and Members of their Families which still has not been enacted. In this new Act/Law all regulations regarding veterans, military invalids and victims of war are going to be incorporated. *See* https://www.paragraf.rs/dnevne-vesti/080519/080519-vest16.html.

Chapter 2. Financial Allowances for the Handicapped

§1. Beneficiaries

377. In terms of the personal field of application, the system of financial protection for handicapped persons in Serbia is highly inclusive. According to Article 6 of the Act on Social Protection 'all citizens' of the RS can be beneficiaries of the financial allowances for the handicapped. Also, foreign citizens and persons without citizenship can be entitled to financial allowances if they reside on the territory of Serbia and if stipulated by this Act, some other Act or by international agreement. The rights are not conditional upon the length of stay within the territory of the country.

378. With regard to military and war invalids, nationality, that is, citizenship, is a pre-condition to becoming entitled to such status. However, the status of being handicapped can also be attained by foreign nationals if they cannot obtain it in their own country, provided that they served their military duty in the defence of the former Yugoslavia (Serbia).

§2. Conditions

379. Conditions for obtaining financial allowances in Serbia depend on the nature of the rights offered. In order for a handicapped person to become entitled to the '*minimum income benefit*', the condition is for him/her to be completely incapacitated to work and not have sufficient means for survival.[299] The degree of incapacity to work is assessed in accordance with the regulations governing benefits arising from industrial accidents and occupational diseases (*see* above).

380. Regarding *allowance for third-party assistance and care*, the condition is that the handicapped person, due to the severity of injury or illness, cannot meet the basic needs for living without assistance. An additional condition is that it is not possible to obtain these benefits on the grounds of some other branch of social security, as well as that the handicapped person is not exercising the right to placement in a social protection institution. Assessment on whether there is a real need for third-party assistance and care is conducted in accordance with the standards set by the branch for industrial accident and occupational disease benefits. The evaluation of the degree to which the requirements to work have been met is conducted by a special committee organized by the Ministry of Labour, Employment, Veterans and Social Affairs.[300] The administration and claims procedures are identical to the procedure to obtain the 'minimum income benefit', which will be explained in more detail further in the text (*see* further).

---

299. *See* Arts 81–84 of the Act on Social Protection.
300. *See* Art. 92 of the Act on Social Protection.

381. A general condition of recognizing the rights of war, military and civilian war invalids is that their handicap occurred at no fault of their own during war or military actions. Each type of handicap carries specific conditions, which are based on the cause of the handicap and degree of disability.[301] On the basis of the degree of the lack of functionality, war and peacetime military invalids are divided into ten categories. Furthermore, each category has a specific level of rights and methods for obtaining the benefits attached.[302]

382. The procedure for assessing the degree of handicap and meeting the requirements for certain entitlements for war veterans, military and civilian war invalids are in Serbia conducted by the municipal or city administration in charge of the protection of veterans and invalids.[303] The procedure itself, as with other social security branches, is conducted as a general administrative proceeding. A person who is not satisfied with the ruling may appeal, and later initiate an administrative dispute before the competent court.[304] As in the cases of other social insurance rights, a change of ruling is possible, as well as a renewal of proceedings if new evidence is presented. Financing for the rights of this group of invalids is provided by the State, and the payments are disbursed monthly.

§3. Benefits

383. Basic financial allowance for handicapped persons in Serbia is the 'minimum income benefit' (actual term used for this right is 'financial social aid'). Since this right, as already mentioned, is only a segment of the general 'minimum income benefit' that applies to all citizens, the methods for its realization will be the topic of next chapter (*see* further). The second financial entitlement – allowance for third-party care and assistance – was set at nominal level of RSD 17,164 (around EUR 145) in 2019, and it is adjusted every six-month to the changes in the consumers' prices, that is, on 1 April and 1 October.[305]

384. Military and war invalids, as determined by the former Federal Act, are entitled to the following financial benefits:

– personal disability allowance;

---

301. For example, a war veteran is a person whose disability equals at least 20%. For peacetime military invalids between 20% and 60%, and civilian war invalids at least 50%.
302. *See* Arts 3–12 of the Act on the Basic Rights of Soldiers, Soldiers with Disabilities and the Families of Soldiers Killed at War.
303. The Regulation on Medical Committees and Their Work has been passed regarding the methods of realizing the rights granted by the Act on the Basic Rights of Soldiers, Soldiers with Disabilities and the Families of Soldiers Killed at War. *See* Official Gazette of the FRY, No. 37/1998, of 27 Jul. 1998.
304. Appeals fall under the competence of the Ministry of Labour, Employment and Social Policy, whereas for Vojvodina it is under the competence of the provincial body in charge of the areas of social protection and veterans' protection. *See* Arts 76–98 of the Act on the Basic Rights of Soldiers, Soldiers with Disabilities and the Families of Soldiers Killed at War.
305. *See* Art. 93 of the Act on Social Protection.

- allowance for assistance and care;
- allowance for orthopaedic auxiliaries;
- unemployment allowance;
- housing and meals allowances.

385. The *personal disability allowance* is determined by the average net earnings in Serbia for the previous month. The basis represents 180% of this amount. The amount of the benefit depends on the degree of invalidity and ranges between 6% and 100%. The *assistance and care allowance* can amount to 46%–100% of the mentioned basis, whereas the *allowance for orthopaedic auxiliaries can amount* to 7%–29% of the basis. An *unemployment allowance* is provided for invalids without income in the amount of the average net earnings in Serbia. *Housing and meals allowances* for the purpose of medical examination or treatment are provided in the amount of real costs.

386. As an addition to these rights, Serbia has established some other means of income for military invalids without financial security. The only condition is that the handicapped person is not entitled to a similar right on other grounds. These additional rights of military invalids are:

- the right to monthly remuneration;[306]
- care allowance;[307]
- compensation for the costs of placement in a social protection institution;
- child allowance (*see* above);
- the right to financial compensation during professional rehabilitation;
- compensation for transportation costs relating to a medical exam or treatment.

Civilian war invalids are not entitled to these particular rights; they are only guaranteed to war and military invalids in accordance with old federal regulations.

306. War veterans, and war and military invalids without financial security are entitled to this benefit. The basis for determining the amount depends on the number of family members and ranges between 14.5% and 66% of the average monthly salary in Serbia, and the amount depends on the income of the handicapped person and ranges between 60% and 80% of the basis. *See* Arts 7–15 of the Act on the Rights of Veterans, Military Invalids and Members of their Families of Serbia (1989).
307. The allowance for care equals 24%–36% of the average monthly salary (in Serbia). *See* Art. 16 of the Act on the Rights of Veterans, Military Invalids and Members of their Families of Serbia.

Part X. Minimum Income Benefit

387. As long ago as 1957, the former SFRY established an all-encompassing system for the protection of the poor (*see* above), which is still applicable almost in a similar form in Serbia. In 2003, Serbia adopted the Poverty Reduction Strategy. Moreover, on 16 December 2005, it adopted a Social Protection Developing Strategy.[308] This developing strategy should reduce the growing rate of poverty in Serbia and, at the same time, it should modernize and make the system of social protection more efficient and more adapted to the needs of vulnerable categories (poor people, invalids, refugees, Roma people, etc.). Some of the goals of the reform of Serbian social protection are de-institutionalization of social protection, development of alternative forms of social protection, and inclusion of private providers and the non-governmental sector into the system of providing services.[309] Majority of these goals were incorporated into the Act on social protection of 4 April 2011.[310] Basic rights have, however, remained almost unchanged.

388. The most important right this social protection system provides is the 'minimum income benefit' (actual term used in Serbian language is 'financial social aid'). In addition, Serbian legislation provides the following material benefits as well:

– allowance for third-party care and assistance (*see* above);
– allowance for training for work (*see* above);
– one-time assistance;
– assistance in goods or services;
– another kind of material benefits (bonuses, free meals in free-meal centres, and similar).[311]

Besides these rights, the Act on Social Protection anticipates a number of 'social protection services'.[312] Since this area is considered to be of particular importance to society, most of the material rights fall under the competence of the Republic.

308. Official Herald of the RS, Nos 108/2005, 75/2005.
309. *See Strategy for Reduction of Poverty in Serbia – Improved Social Protection* (Strategija za smanjenje siromaštva u Srbiji – Efikasnija socijalna zaštita), Romski Informativni Centar (RIC), Internet: www.ric.org.yu/cms/images/bilteni/bilten%20br6.pdf/ (2008).
310. Official Herald of the RS, No. 24/2011.
311. *See* Arts 79–112 of the Act on Social Protection.
312. According to Art. 40 of the Act on Social Protection, there are several branches of social protection services: (1) services in evaluation and planning (assessment of the existing conditions, present

However, some entitlements, which are easier to organize efficiently at the local level, as well as additional benefits, are left under the jurisdiction of the individual cities or municipalities.[313]

389. The opportunity to exercise social security rights is provided by a widespread network of various social protection institutions. Among them, the most important institution in Serbia is the 'social work centre', which, among other duties, makes decisions regarding all social protection rights. Social work centres, organized at the level of municipalities, function as the link between the State, beneficiaries and institutions within the system of social protection. Additionally, there are specialized institutions of social protection that provide particular services within the system of social protection (such as children and youth welfare institutions, abodes/homes, reception centres, foster care and adoption centres, social health institutions).[314] The prevailing number of these institutions are operated by the State, but some can be founded by private individuals as well (not the social work centres, and children and youth welfare institutions, however, because they are considered to be institutions of particular importance to society). These institutions have to obtain the work permit, that is, licence which verifies that it met the required standards needed for its operation in this field (proctor, personnel, etc.).[315] The licence is issued for the period of six years by the Ministry of Labour, Employment, Veterans and Social Affairs.

needs, possibilities and risks to which beneficiaries and their family members are exposed), (2) services provided in/by the community on daily bases (day care, assistance at home and other family and in-home services, (3) assistance in independent living (*see* above), (4) counselling/therapeutic and social /educational services, (5) providing accommodation services (arranging accommodation with relatives, in foster homes, boarding houses, shelter homes, and similar).

313. Social protection services and one-time assistance are financed from the budgets of local communities (by the municipality or the city). *See* Arts 206–209 of the Act on Social Protection.
314. Apart from these institutions, there is the Social Protection Bureau which executes various development, counselling, research and similar tasks. The Bureau is founded by the Republic or the Autonomous Province. *See* Arts 10, 14–18 and 119–134 of the Act on Social Protection.
315. *See* Arts 178–184 of the Act on Social Protection.

Chapter 1. Beneficiaries

390. As previously mentioned, according to the Act on Social Protection, the rights governing the area of social protection (among these, financial security) are provided to all citizens of the Republic that do not have sufficient resources for survival. This includes foreigners as well as persons without citizenship who legally reside within the territory of the Republic, regardless of the length of their stay.

The right to financial security covers individuals who live alone or in families.[316]

316. Around 270,000 persons in Serbia were entitled to financial security in 2018. *See*, *Broj korisnika socijalne pomoći se ne smanjuje (The Number of Social Assistance Beneficiaries Does Not Decrease)*, RTS (Television news portal – Radio Televizije Srbije), 17 Oct. 2018, http://www.rts.rs /page/stories/sr/story/125/drustvo/3292430/broj-korisnika-socijalne-pomoci-se-ne-smanjuje.html.

Chapter 2. Conditions

391. There are a few different ways of fulfilling the conditions to qualify for financial security. The first option refers to individuals or families whose members are incapacitated to work, while left without means of support. The other option is that a person cannot otherwise secure sufficient means to meet basic needs (e.g., on the basis of work, from relatives who are obliged to provide support, on the basis of property and property rights).

392. Individuals or families are considered to have insufficient means if their income is below the base 'minimum income benefit' as prescribed by the Act. When determining allocation of the benefit, the amount of RSD 8,508 (about EUR 72) is taken as the base. The amount is adjusted every six months to the changes in the consumers' prices (on 1 April and 1 October).[317]

393. When assessing the capability of making an income, the following factors are considered:

- income;
- ownership of property or other material rights;
- willingness to work;
- resources of relatives.

The following types of incomes for a person or family are taken into account:

- income and earnings on a monthly bases;
- income from agricultural activities;
- income from leasing movable and fixed assets;
- income from other property rights, if the income is taxable;
- income from unemployment benefit;
- redundancy payment.[318]

Some resources are not taken into account:

- child allowance and birth grant;
- third-party assistance and care allowance;
- compensation for bodily harm;
- awards money and pension severance pay;
- financial aid on the grounds of student status (scholarships and credits);
- free shares for employees;

317. *See* Arts 87–89 of the Act on Social Protection.

318. *See* Arts 82 and 83 of the Act on Social Protection. The Regulation on income and other earnings related to acquisition of the rights to financial and social aid was brought on 27 May 2011 (Official Herald of the RS, No. 36/2011). *See* Arts 2–10). The regulations administering social security in Serbia can be seen at: https://www.minrzs.gov.rs/sr/dokumenti/zakoni/sektor-za-brigu-o-porodici-i-socijalnu-zastitu/zakon-o-socijalnoj-zastiti-i.

- financial aid for basic and any form of additional training as well as for setting up a line of business;
- occasional financial aid received by certain categories of individuals for the purposes of improving their standard of living.[319]

An income determined in this manner is then decreased by the amount that must be paid for the mandatory support of persons who do not live with the family, that is, for alimony payments.

394. One of the criteria for minimum income benefit is willingness to work. The law requires the applicant to show willingness to work. If he/she does not work, the reasons for unemployment must be justified:

- that they are incapacitated to work;
- that they are not performing any business activities;
- that they do not attend school or professional training;
- that they are registered with the employment Fund and have not refused any offers to work, nor to engage in temporary, occasional or seasonal jobs, and that they have not refused professional development courses, vocational re-training or primary education;
- that their employment has not been terminated by their own will, consent or fault;
- that he/she looks after his/her disabled child and therefore cannot be employed.[320]

395. Property or capital ownership is also taken into account. In this case, the individual or family shall be entitled to financial security provided that:

- in addition to living quarters to suit the need of individuals, that is families (one room per family member, or two rooms for individuals receiving the third-party assistance and care allowance) and a plot covering up to 0.5 hectares, no other fixed assets are owned;[321]
- the individual, that is family member, has not sold, given away or repudiated the right to inherit fixed assets;

---

319. According to the Act on Social Protection (Art. 89, para. 3) the income to be exempted should be determined by the Government of Serbia. This issue was regulated by the said Act on allowances and income to be taken into account when determining the eligibility for financial and social aid (Arts 11 and 12). *See* Arts 89 and 212 of the Act on Social Protection.
320. *See* Art. 83 of the Act on Social Protection.
In order to stimulate individuals receiving financial and social aid to be more proactive and step out of the permanent social isolation, on 14 Oct. 2014 the Government of the Republic of Serbia brought The Regulation on Measures for Social Inclusion of the Beneficiaries of Financial Social Aid, (Official Herald of the RS, No. 112/2014.
321. Unless consent has been given to register mortgage rights until settlement of evaluated costs provided on the basis of the right to financial security.

– a period of time has lapsed during which they could, from the market value of the fixed asset that has been transferred, or for which they have repudiated the right to inherit, provide financial security;
– the individual does not own movable assets by use, or sale, of which they might provide resources equalling six times the amount of financial security without jeopardizing their basic needs;
– the individual is not covered by a lifetime support contract.[322]

Savings deposits, money, securities and the value of other transferred estates are all considered to be income from property or property rights.

396. The right to financial security may also be realized by individuals, that is, families, who do not meet the cited requirements if they authorize the social work centres to mortgage the property, or part of the property and to have the financial security paid from these resources.

397. With individuals incapacitated to work, it is also taken into account whether there are persons (relatives) who are mandated to support them. In accordance with the regulations on marriage and family, these include parents, grandparents, step-parents, children and grandchildren, step-children and siblings. Unless already ordered to do so by the court, these persons may be designated by the social work centre to provide support for the incapacitated individual, instead of financial security or its part.[323]

322. *See* Art. 82 of the Act on Social Protection.
323. *See* Art. 84 of the Act on Social Protection.

Chapter 3. Amount of Benefit

398. The amount of financial security is not linear, but represents the difference between the previously set base of 'minimum income benefit' (*see* above) and the average monthly income of the individual or the family, as realized in the preceding three months. However, the base for the benefit is not linear; it changes according to the number of family members and their age. For the holder of the benefit in the family, the base is 1, providing that an additional 0.5 of the base is added for each family member (i.e., 0.3 for each family member under 18 years of age). Compensation is paid on a monthly basis. The benefit can be increased up to 20% in cases when the minimum income benefit is received by a person incapable to work, or a family in which all members are incapable to work, or a single-parent family.[324]

324. *See* Arts 87–90 of the Act on Social Protection.

Chapter 4. Claims and Administration

399. The administration of the minimum income benefit in Serbia has been entrusted to social work centres that are mostly organized at the community level. These centres deal with issues relating to the rights in all areas of social protection. The request is to be submitted to the social work centre responsible for the territory on which the underprivileged person resides. When filling the form, the applicant for material benefit must provide true and full data. He/she will, otherwise, be held liable for compensation of the damage.

400. The procedure to realize the rights provided for in this law is conducted according to the rules of the general administrative proceedings. In the first instance, the case has to be concluded within sixty days. It is interesting to note that the social work centre, when deciding on this or some other social assistance rights, is authorized to replace one right with another against the will of the beneficiary. The centre can do this if it finds this solution to be in the interest of the beneficiary or the public, provided that the person is incapable to work.[325]

401. An appeal against the social work centre's decision can be filed within thirty days from the day the decision was passed by the Ministry of Labour, Employment, Veterans and Social Affairs (for the territory of Vojvodina, it is the provincial secretariat that has jurisdiction for social protection issues). After that, an administrative dispute may be initiated before the Administrative Court within thirty days.

325. *See* Arts 69 and 95–106 of the Act on Social Protection.

Chapter 5. Reclaiming of Benefits Paid

402. Improvement in a beneficiary's financial situation affects the benefit. The beneficiary, his/her legal representative or guardian is under the obligation to report to the social work centre every change that might influence the entitlement within fifteen days of the change. Also, the social work centre has to re-evaluate the conditions for exercising the financial security rights every year (in May).

403. Paid benefits can be reclaimed if the applicant realizes this right:

- on the grounds of false and incorrect data which they were aware of, or should have been aware of, at the time of submission of application;
- if they have otherwise realized this benefit, even though they were not entitled to it or if they realized it at a larger scale than entitled to;
- if they fail to report a change that would cause the loss of right or decrease the amount of right, while they were aware, or should have been aware, of the change.[326]

The law does not contain the provision of what happens when a material error is committed without the applicant's awareness. It can only be assumed that in that case the benefit is not returned.

326. Within a month after publishing official statistics about salary variations in the first quarter of the current year. *See* Arts 96–97 and 105 of the Act on Social Protection.

Part XI. Claims and Adjudication

Chapter 1. Claims

§1. Introduction of Claims

404. The general principle in Serbian law is that beneficiaries can obtain entitlement to benefits only if they come forward and make a claim. Only on rare occasions do social security institutions decide on the rights of beneficiaries on their own accord. Such decisions are usually made in the area of social assistance (protection) to the poor and handicapped and in the area of child protection.

405. A benefits claim need not be submitted in any particular form, but it must contain all necessary evidence and documentation.[327] In addition, the claim must be made within a certain time frame and submitted to the competent institution. In most branches, the entitlement is lost when the claim is made more than three years following the event giving rise to the right. In the employment branch, the deadline is particularly short. The claim must be made within the period for which the insured person would have the right to unemployment benefits. The claims are not paid for the elapsed time (*see* above). In the branch covering pensions, the right to make a claim is not limited by time; however, back payments can be made only for the six months prior to the claim if the claim was made late.

406. Social security rights are decided in special administrative proceedings, called the 'general administrative proceedings'. These proceedings are always undertaken when State organs and other public services or institutions decide on civil rights. They are regulated by the Act on General Administrative Proceedings of 1 March 2016.[328] The Act, among other things, states certain important rights related to the making of decisions on social security rights:

- the duty for institutions to motivate decisions;
- the duty to mention the possibility of appeal, the duty to pass erroneous applications on to the competent institution;

327. Standard forms allowing a person to fill in the required data have been recently made and used frequently.
328. The Central Social Insurance Register is not yet in function. Published in the Official Gazette of the FRY, Nos 33/1997, 31/2001 and Official Herald of the RS, Nos 3018/20102016, 95/2018.

– the duty to decide upon an application within thirty or sixty days at the latest;[329]
– the duty to decide on an appeal within sixty days.[330]

The protection of the privacy of the beneficiaries in the proceedings is not mentioned in legislation. However, it is implied on a constitutional basis and on the basis of the Act on Personal Data Protection of 27 October 2008.[331] Based on that, on 6 April 2013, the Minister of Labour, Employment and Social Policy adopted the Regulation on keeping, protection and safety of data stored in the information system of the Central registry of beneficiaries of obligatory social security.[332] This Act was brought in order to prevent unauthorized use of information on beneficiaries of social security and protection of the privacy of the beneficiaries of the social security system.[333]

407. With regard to social security benefits in practice, a problem arises related to the sheer number of documents necessary to claim a benefit, and in some branches they need to be updated periodically (e.g., in the area of family allowances, every six months). The difficulty in obtaining these documents still exists despite the fact that the Central Social Insurance Register is available since 2008.[334] In other words, while applying for the benefit, candidates have to submit documents that are not stored in Central Register. However, during the last few years a universal information system containing the most important data has been installed in the majority of social security institutions, thus allowing faster completion of granting procedure.

408. The benefits should be paid without delay, during the month following the decision. However, in practice, as a result of the financial crisis in the 1990s, there have been long delays in both making decisions, and more importantly, in disbursing benefits in almost all branches of social security. Payment disparities were largely reduced during 2001 and 2002, owing to foreign donations, but the late payments have not included interest accrued. There are still occasional slight delays in benefit payments in most branches (sickness benefit, maternity benefit, child allowance, unemployment benefit).[335]

---

329. *See* Art. 145 of the Act. This principle is often observed in practice. For example, when making decisions/rulings with regard to pensions, the decision-making process can last for up to four or five months, during which period the insured person does not have access to any means of subsistence.
330. *See* Art. 174 of the Act.
331. Official Herald of the RS, Nos 97/2008, 104/2009, 68/2012, 107/2012.
332. Official Herald of the RS, No. 29/2013.
333. *See* Arts 2 and 3 of the Regulation.
334. *See* the Act on Central Register of Social Insurance of 8 Dec. 2018 (Official Herald of the RS, No. 95/2018).
335. For example, during 2002 only 10.5 instead of 12 pensions were paid in Serbia. *See also*: *Porodiljske naknade kasne, a zavise od poslodavaca (Maternity Benefits Are Late, and Depend on Employers),* 021 (Informative portal), 19 Jan. 2019, https://www.021.rs/story/Info/Srbija/206203/Porodiljske-naknade-kasne-a-zavise-od-poslodavaca.html.

§2. Protection Against Seizure and Transfer

409. The matter of seizure and transferability of social benefits in Serbia is regulated by the Act on Executive Proceedings and Collection of 21 December 2015.[336] In accordance with Article 257 of that Act, some of the benefits in the area of social security are fully protected against seizure and transfer. These are:

- compensation for damages resulting from health impairment, diminished or loss of capacity to work;
- income based on benefits resulting from bodily harm;
- minimum income benefit and other allowances on the basis of social security;
- unemployment allowance;
- child allowance.

410. Pensions and other benefits from social insurance are treated as wages. These incomes can be suspended only to the level of the two-thirds of benefit (half, if the person is receiving minimal wage).[337]

411. Pensions and the incomes of war and military invalids can be suspended only in the event of claims made on the basis of legal support, compensation for damages resulting from health impairment, diminished or loss of capacity to work and due to the loss of support benefits resulting from the death of the benefit provider. In the event of benefit seizure or transfer, the beneficiary must be entitled to a minimum of half of the benefit.[338]

Deductions in social security benefits cannot be applied ex officio. The institution and claimant must obtain a court order.

§3. Legal Capacity to Receive Benefits

412. In accordance with the regulations in civil law, the rule is that the legal capacity to receive benefits is dependent on the beneficiary's full capacity to work. The rights with regard to the possibility of receiving benefits are equal among genders. The Regulations on family law does not allow for the possibility that a spouse can ask for a court order to receive certain benefits if the other spouse behaves in a fiscally irresponsible manner with his/her benefits.[339]

413. For young persons who are not yet of age to receive benefits in their own right (under 18 years of age), benefits are disbursed to the parents. If a child is either in the care of another person or in an institution, then this caregiver will receive the benefits that the child is entitled to. There are cases when benefit payments are

336. Published in the Official Herald of the RS, Nos 106/2015, 106/2016, 113/2017.
337. *See* Art. 258 of the Act on Executive Proceedings.
338. *See* Art. 258, para. 4 of the Act on Executive Proceedings.
339. There is only a possibility of work capacity deprivation. *See* Arts 146–150 The Family Law in Serbia, on 24 Feb. 2005, Official Herald of the RS, Nos 18/2005, 72/2011, 6/2015.

reduced or suspended for the period when financial benefits, hospital treatment and placement with other families or institutions are financed by the State, that is, by social security institutions.[340]

340. For instance, in accordance with Art. 212, para. 6 of the Act on Social Protection, third-person care and assistance allowance is considered to be the beneficiary's income when determining participation in costs of day care and assistance at home.

Chapter 2. Adjudication

414. The competence of the courts with regard to disputes in the area of social security in Serbia has been determined by laws of each branch of social security, as well as by special law on the court system – the Act on Courts Settlements of 22 December 2008.[341] Such disputes are resolved mainly by the Administrative Court in a special court procedure called an administrative dispute.

415. A majority of disputes in the area of social insurance in Serbia are heard in the 'Administrative Court' and exceptionally, by Higher – district courts.[342] In exceptional circumstances, disputes in health insurance are heard in basic courts, in a regular civil procedure and not in an administrative dispute.[343] The same procedure is followed in disputes arising from the employer's failure to make payment against the contribution for the insurance of employees. There is another exception. On extraordinary legal remedies for the decisions made by other courts and for 'request for revision of the decision' brought by administrative court, the competent court is the Supreme Cassation Court of Serbia.[344]

416. Judicial procedure in the administrative dispute hearing in Serbia has been regulated by the Act on Administrative Disputes of 29 December 2009.[345] An administrative dispute is a special type of judicial procedure that reconsiders acts introduced by State administrations, public services and social security institutions that have made decisions on individual civil rights. A party is entitled to initiate an administrative dispute within thirty days of receiving a decision regarding his/her rights or within sixty days if the appellate organ has not ruled on its appeal. The trial is usually conducted without the presence of the parties, except when necessary in order to establish evidence. The flaws of this procedure are its lengthiness when resolving cases, and the fact that the individual who introduces the appeal against a social security institution is not exempt from covering the court costs. In other words, the rule states that each party must cover his/her expenses (taxes, lawyers, experts). In exceptional circumstances, the individual who introduces the appeal can be exempted from such payment if unable to cover the court costs due to poverty.[346]

341. Official Herald of the RS, Nos 116/2008, 104/2009, 101/2010, 31/2011, 78/2011, 101/2011, 101/2013, 40/2015, 106/2015, 13/2016, 108/2016, 113/2017, 65/2018, 87/2018, 88/2018.
342. According to Art. 23, para. 1, subpara. 8, of the Act, the higher court shall adjudicate on disputes concerning compulsory social security if it is not competent for another court; *See* Arts 23 and 29 of the Act on Courts Settlement.
343. Only in case of compensation for the damages and if there is a lawsuit against the medical institution which provided medical treatment to, or deprived the insured of it.
344. *See* Art. 30 of the Act on Courts Settlement of 2008 and Art. 49 of the Act on Administrative Disputes of 2009 (*see* further).
345. Official Herald of the RS, No. 111/2009.
346. This segment of the judicial procedure is subsidiary governed by the Act on Civil Procedure of 28 Sep. 2011 (Official Herald of the RS, Nos 72/2011, 49/2013, 74/2013, 55/2014, 87/2018). *See* Arts 168–169 of the Act.

Selected Bibliography

§1. Legislation

Službeni list državne zajednice Srbije i Crne Gore (The Official Gazette of the State Union of Serbia and Montenegro), the means of official publication of federal laws and other regulations, Belgrade.

Službeni glasnik Republike Srbije (The Official Herald of the Republic of Serbia), the means of official publication of laws and other regulations to be applied in the Republic of Serbia, Belgrade.

Službeni list Savezne Republike Jugoslavije (The Official Gazette of the Federal Republic of Yugoslavia), the means of official publication of federal laws and other regulations, Belgrade.

§2. Reviews of Court Decisions

Bilten sudske prakse (Bulletin of Court Rulings). Belgrade: Supreme Cassation Court, the Official Gazette.

Bilten sudske prakse (Bulletin of Court Rulings). Belgrade: The First Municipal Court, the Department of Court Rulings.

Izbor sudske prakse (A Selection of Court Rulings). Belgrade: Glosarijum.

Penzijsko-invalidsko, zdravstveno osiguranje i zdravstvena zaštita – sudska praksa i mišljenja nadležnih ministarstava (Pension and Disability Insurance, Health Insurance and Health Protection – Court Rulings and Opinions of Appropriate Ministries). Court and Administrative Rulings 1998, No. 2.

Pravna praksa (Legal Practice). Belgrade: Liber.

Registar važe ih propisa sa sudskom praksom (Register of Current Regulations with Court Rulings). Belgrade: Savremena administracija.

Sudska praksa (Court Rulings). Zemun: Poslovna politika.

Vrhovni kasacioni sud (Supreme Cassation Court), www.vk.sud.rs/sudska-praksa.html.

Upravni sud Beograd (Administrative Court Belgrade), http://www.up.sud.rs/english/jurisprudence-of-the-administrative-court.

Apelacioni sud u Beogradu (Court of Appeal in Belgrade), http://www.bg.ap.sud.rs/lt/articles/sudska-praksa/pregled-sudske-prakse-apelacionog-suda-u-beogradu/odeljenje-radnih-sporova/r1-49-10.html.

Apelacioni sud u Novom Sadu (Court of Appeal in Novi Sad), http://www.ns.ap.sud.rs/index.php/src/sudska-praksa.

Apelacioni sud u Nišu (Court of Appeal in Nish), http://www.ni.ap.sud.rs/pageView.do?id_strane=104.
Apelacioni sud u Kragujevcu (Court of Appeal in Kragujevac), http://www.kg.ap.sud.rs/sudska-praksa.html.

§3. Books

Baltić, A. & M. Despotović. *Osnovi radnog prava Jugoslavije i osnovni problemi sociologije rada* (*Fundaments of Labour Law of Yugoslavia and the Basic Problems of the Sociology of Labour*). Belgrade: Savremena Administracija, 1971.
Brajić, V. *Radno pravo* (*Labour Law*). Belgrade: Savremena Administracija, 2001.
Gojković G. *Socijalno osiguranje, zdravstvena i socijalna zaštita* (*Social Insurance, Health and Social Protection*). Belgrade: Zaštita Rada, 1985.
Golubović, V. *Finansiranje penzijskog i invalidskog osiguranja* (*Financing of Pension and Invalidity Insurance*). Novi Sad: Budućnost, 2002.
Jašarević, S. *Socijalno pravo (Social Law).* Novi Sad: Pravni fakultet, Univerzitet u Novom Sadu, 2010.
Jelčić, V. *Socijalno pravo u SFRJ, knjiga 1. Socijalno osiguranje* (*Social Law in SFRY, Book 1.Social Insurance*). Zagreb: Informator, 1988.
Jovanović, P. *Radno pravo* (*Labour Law*). Novi Sad: Pravni fakultet, 2015.
Jovanović, P. & D. Nešskov. *Zdravstvena zašstita i zdravstveno osiguranje* (*Health Protection and Health Insurance*). Novi Sad: Dnevnik, 1989.
Kaclerović, T. *Radno zakonodavstvo u Srbiji – pre I svetskog rata* (*Labour Legislation in Serbia – Prior to World War I*). Belgrade: Narodna knjiga, 1952.
Lazarević, R. & T. Vujošević. *Socijalno osiguranje u Jugoslaviji* (*Social Insurance in Yugoslavia*). Belgrade: Kultura, 1958.
Munćan, J. *Socijalno pravo* (*Social Law*). Novi Sad: Univerzitet u Novom Sadu, 1999.
Perić, B. *Radno pravo FNRJ* (*Labour Law of the FPRY*). Sarajevo: Odbor za izdavanje udžbenika i skripata za studente univerziteta i visokihšskola NR BiH, 1950.
Petrović, A. *Starosne penzije (socijalno osiguranje)* (*Old-Age Pensions – Social Insurance*). Belgrade: Naučna Knjiga, 1991.
Pešić, R. *Nastanak i razvitak socijalnog osiguranja u Jugoslaviji I i II* (*The Inception and Development of Social Insurance in Yugoslavia*). Belgrade: Savezni Zavod Za Socijalno Osiguranje, 1957.
Pešsić, R. *Radno pravo, knjiga III – Socijalno osiguranje* (*Labour Law, Book III – Social Insurance*). Novi Sad: Pravni Fakultet u Novom Sadu, 1975.
Statistical Yearbook of Yugoslavia 2001. Federal Statistical Office, 2002.
Stojanović, Lj. & V. Stošsić.*Zbirka medjuunarodnih ugovora o socijalnom osiguranju* (*A Collection of International Treaties on Social Insurance*). Belgrade: Zašstita Rada, 1996.
Šunderi, B. *Socijalno pravo (Social Law),* Belgrade: Pravni fakultet Univerziteta u Beogradu, 2009.
Vajs, E. *Socijalno obezbedjenje – u Jugoslaviji, 9ešskoj,ŠSvedskoj i Velikoj Britaniji* (*Social Security – In Yugoslavia, the Czech Republic, Sweden and UK*). Belgrade: Institut Za Medunarodnu Politiku i Privredu, 1960.

Vuković, D. *Socijalno obezbedjenje* (*Social Security*). Kraljevo: Centar Za Socijalni Rad, 1994.
Vuković, D. *Socijalna sigurnost i socijalna prava* (*Social Security and Social Rights*). Belgrade: Savez Drušstava Socijalnih Radnika, 1999.
Vuković, D. *Socijalna sigurnost i socijalna prava* (*Social Security and Social Rights*). Belgrade: Fakultet politickih nauka Univerziteta u Beogradu, 2005.

§4. Periodicals (Journals)

Radno i socijalno pravo (*Labour and Social Law*). Belgrade: Udruženje Za Radno i Socijalno Pravo Srbije.
Socijalno pravo (*Social Law*). Belgrade: Udruženje Pravnika Za Socijalno Osiguranje.
Socijalna misao (Social Doctrine). Belgrade: Republički zavod za socijalnu zaštitu i Socijalna misao.
Bilten sudske prakse (Bulletin of Court Rulings). Belgrade: Supreme Cassation Court, the Official Gazette.
Bilten sudske prakse (Bulletin of Court Rulings). Belgrade: The First Municipal Court, the Department of Court Rulings.
Izbor sudske prakse (A Selection of Court Rulings). Belgrade: Glosarijum.
Penzijsko-invalidsko, zdravstveno osiguranje i zdravstvena zaštita – sudska praksa i mišljenja nadležnih ministarstava (Pension and Disability Insurance, Health Insurance and Health Protection – Court Rulings and Opinions of Appropriate Ministries). Court and Administrative Rulings 1998, No. 2.
Pravna praksa (Legal Practice). Belgrade: Liber.
Registar važe ih propisa sa sudskom praksom (Register of Current Regulations with Court Rulings). Belgrade: Savremena administracija.
Sudska praksa (Court Rulings). Zemun: Poslovna politika.
Vrhovni kasacioni sud (Supreme Cassation Court), www.vk.sud.rs/sudska-praksa.html.
Upravni sud Beograd (Administrative Court Belgrade), http://www.up.sud.rs/english/jurisprudence-of-the-administrative-court.
Apelacioni sud u Beogradu (Court of Appeal in Belgrade), http://www.bg.ap.sud.rs/lt/articles/sudska-praksa/pregled-sudske-prakse-apelacionog-suda-u-beogradu/odeljenje-radnih-sporova/r1-49-10.html.
Apelacioni sud u Novom Sadu (Court of Appeal in Novi Sad), http://www.ns.ap.sud.rs/index.php/src/sudska-praksa.
Apelacioni sud u Nišu (Court of Appeal in Nish), http://www.ni.ap.sud.rs/pageView.do?id_strane=104.
Apelacioni sud u Kragujevcu (Court of Appeal in Kragujevac), http://www.kg.ap.sud.rs/sudska-praksa.html.

Selected Bibliography

Index

The numbers here refer to paragraph numbers.

www.ingramcontent.com/pod-product-compliance
Ingram Content Group UK Ltd.
Pitfield, Milton Keynes, MK11 3LW, UK
UKHW020145290926
15471UKWH00004B/704

9 789403 526027